The American 1960s

It used to be that way
Now it goes like this

                              —BOB DYLAN, 1965

The American 1960s

Imaginative Acts in a Decade of Change

Jerome Klinkowitz

The Iowa State University Press, Ames

1 9 8 0

Jerome Klinkowitz is Professor of English at the University of Northern Iowa. He is the author of *The Practice of Fiction in America: Writers from Hawthorne to the Present* (1980); *The Life of Fiction* (1977); and *Literary Disruptions* (1975; revised, 1980); co-author of *Vonnegut in America* (1977) and *The Vonnegut Statement* (1973); compiler of the descriptive bibliographies *Donald Barthelme* (1977) and *Kurt Vonnegut* (1974); and editor of *The Diaries of Willard Motley* (1979), *Writing Under Fire* (1978), and *Innovative Fiction* (1972). His art criticism has appeared in the Chicago *Tribune, Kritikon Litterarum* (Köln), and *Revue Française d'Etudes Américaines* (Paris); and as a rock musician he has recorded and toured with *Junior & the Classics* and *The Del Reys* (in the sixties) and *Raggs* (in the seventies).

© 1980 The Iowa State University Press. All rights reserved

Composed and printed by The Iowa State University Press, Ames, Iowa 50010

First edition, 1980

For permission to include material published by them, grateful acknowledgement is made to the following:

Alfred A. Knopf, Inc., for permission to quote from *The Collected Poems of Frank O'Hara,* ed. Donald Allen. Copyright © 1971 by Maureen Granville-Smith, Administratrix of the Estate of Frank O'Hara.

Farrar, Straus & Giroux, Inc., for permission to quote from *Life Studies,* Robert Lowell. Copyright © 1956, 1959 by Robert Lowell.

City Lights Books for permission to quote from "The Day Lady Died," Frank O'Hara. Copyright © 1964 by Frank O'Hara.

Library of Congress Cataloging in Publication Data

Klinkowitz, Jerome.
  The American 1960s.

  Includes index.
  1. American fiction—20th century—History and Criticism.   2. United States—civilization—1945-
I. Title.
PS379.K546   813′.009   80-11943
ISBN 0-8138-1380-8

CONTENTS

for Julie Huffman-Klinkowitz

PREFACE

It seems only a habit of popular culture that twentieth-century Americans have tended to define their experience of decades with the symbolic identities scholars reserve for centuries. Yet cultural and literary critics have adopted these mini-epochs as useful distinctions for their own more serious works. Hence the progress of titles covering the past eighty years, from Larzer Ziff's *The American 1890s: Life and Times of a Lost Generation,* Malcolm Cowley's anthology *After the Genteel Tradition* (on the decades surrounding World War I), Frederick Hoffman's monumental *The Twenties,* and Frederick Lewis Allen's popular *Only Yesterday* to Leo Gurko's *The Angry Decade* (on the thirties), Chester Eisinger's *Fiction of the Forties,* Daniel Bell's *The End of Ideology* (on fifties intellectual culture), and, most recently, Morris Dickstein's *Gates of Eden: American Culture of the Sixties.*

The American 1960s reflects this critical tradition, not withstanding the regrettable fact that, in some recent critical analyses, labels are placed upon decades indiscriminately, as if each ten-year period had equal effect in developing the country's culture. The twenties, of course, are now remembered as a great period of innovation in literature (including the birth of popular modernism through the work of F. Scott Fitzgerald, Ernest Hemingway, and William Faulkner) while the thirties made the arts a utilitarian concern in the face of social and political reforms. Do the forties and fifties merit the same epochal coverage? Most likely not, and suspicion of such works which try to rank the achievements of recent decades with, say, the twenties, has served to discredit this approach.

But the sixties unquestionably merit such treatment. A wealth of circumstantial facts help square away the dates: from the promise of John Kennedy's 1961 inauguration to the death of the American protest movement after Richard Nixon's invasion of Cambodia and the killings at Kent State; from the conservativism of theme and form in fifties fiction to the success of topically radical and structurally innovative books by Kurt Vonnegut, Richard Brautigan, and Donald Barthelme which closed the decade; and most apparently from the changes in popular music, personal behavior, and human values which took place between 1960 and 1970. As for the cultural change itself, the effects are obvious. All that ask to be explained are the causes.

Mere accumulation of data does not make a thesis, much less prove one. But a beginning can be made by selecting a very few decisive acts from a sample of behavior and showing how their imaginative form reveals a systematic change which permeates the decade's culture. Changes in the American imagination are at its root, and how that imagination exercised itself in different contexts is this book's subject. For example, once a political figure such as John Fitzgerald Kennedy has made his impression on the general conduct of life, he may live on in persons' imaginations just as much as fictional characters—a Yossarian, McMurphy, or Billy Pilgrim. Persons manage reality by their constructions; and from John Kennedy to Billy Pilgrim, Americans in the 1960s were offered strikingly new ways to put things together. Thus to see the real character of these models for change one can look at Kennedy, for instance, in literary terms, while such literary craftsmen as Vonnegut and Ken Kesey may be studied for their historical and even political suggestions. Kennedy and McMurphy each are new constructs in people's minds, new ways of shaping the world. The political image of John Kennedy, the fictional devices of Joseph Heller, Ken Kesey, and Kurt Vonnegut, and the melodies of Neil Young and Bob Dylan—all are instances of a new imaginative approach to the world, *a new idea* of one sort or another. What characterizes the American 1960s is that all these proffered constructs came about at roughly the same time; that they reflected a similar imaginative ideal; and that they persist in ongoing American culture as icons of the decade even in the minds of those who have since rejected that very ideal.

Everything important to the sixties, of course, did not happen exclusively within the decade's dates. It was in the first half of the 1960s, for example, that the Civil Rights movement came to its triumphs of news media attention, broadly based popular support, and legislative reform— but only as the climax of a struggle with immediate roots in the forties and fifties and a long history dating back through Reconstruction, Emancipation, Abolition, and enslavement itself. The early sixties are also the climax of a twenty-year period in which black American music—jazz, blues, and especially rhythm and blues—slowly reshaped the commercially popular song. But the tragedy is that most of the great composers and musicians who were immediately influential upon the sixties—bluesmen Robert Johnson and Huddie Ledbetter, singers Bessie Smith and Billie Holiday, jazzmen Charlie Parker and Clifford Brown—were dead before the decade began. Hence a book on the American 1960s is a study, not of their original art, but of how it influenced a decade's thinking. July 17, 1959, is the date of Billie Holiday's death, but as "The Day Lady Died" it is also the title of one of Frank O'Hara's most revealing poems—revealing how the coming decade would alter its values and perception of life. Yet popular styles can be fickle things, and it is to this country's great shame that only in the seventies did black artists in any great numbers begin receiving full critical and financial credit for their contributions to American culture. And only in the seventies did serious studies and debates of "the black aesthetic" get underway.

But from a selection of popularly effective figures within the decade, including presidents, poets, and rock stars, the reader may catch hold of the spirit of an age. For the sixties especially, when the news media made accountability a prime requisite of authority, there was a reinforcement between how these figures reacted to contemporary reality and how it reacted to them. Only by studying both may a start be made toward defining the American 1960s.

ACKNOWLEDGMENTS

Contemporary studies, and in particular the discussion of the American 1960s, remains a controversial topic, and therefore I am grateful for the exceptional support given me by the University of Northern Iowa (including a semester's Professional Development Leave) and several universities abroad.

Much of this book was developed in lectures, seminars, and informal discussions during three months spent in France, Hungary, and Poland during 1978 and 1979. The perspective Europe offers on American matters has been obvious since the temporary emigrations of F. Scott Fitzgerald and Ernest Hemingway. But in our own day and for my particular subject, there is a special advantage. Because of the time lag in translations, literary works of the American 1960s have become widely available to European readers only in the 1970s. Hence the discussion of Kesey, Heller, and Vonnegut—even of Kennedy and Nixon—remains fresh and vital, while the American critic can benefit from ten years' hindsight.

It is the perfect environment for the study of my theme, and hence I wish to thank Professors André Le Vot, Marc Chenetier, and Régis Durand of the Centre de Recherche sur la Littérature Américaine Contemporaine, Université de Paris-III (Sorbonne Nouvelle), Professor Franciszek Lyra and Mr. Jerzy Kutnik of Maria Curie-Skłodowska University (Lublin), Professor Marta Sienicka and Mr. Janusz Semrau of Adam Mickiewicz University (Posnan), Professor Zbigniew Lewicki (University of Warsaw), Messrs. Ernö Kulcsár-Szabó and Ákos Szilágyi of Budapest, and Professors Zoltán Abádi-Nagy and Zoltan Szilássy of Kossuth Lajos University (Debrecen) for arranging my visits and for hours of helpful discussion. Jerzy Kutnik, Zoltán Abádi-Nagy, and Zoltán Szilassy read an earlier version of this manuscript and offered good advice; at the Iowa State University Press Suzanne C. Lowitt made eminently helpful suggestions in matters both of substance and of style, complementing earlier critiques by Rowena James Malone and Raymond Fassel. For all their help I am most grateful, since much of what may be worthwhile is to their credit, while the imperfections are my own.

JEROME KLINKOWITZ

Astoria Hotel, Budapest
October 1979

THE AMERICAN 1960s

CHAPTER ONE

Kennedy and Nixon: Images as Fictions

The new circumstances of American life demand new words, new phrases, and the transfer of old words to new objects—so said Thomas Jefferson as the United States began. Few challenged Jefferson's argument that a new age was at hand; the American wilderness had been colonized in the previous century by a people moved by specific economic and spiritual purposes, and now a group of rationalist statesmen were setting it on an explicitly new political course as well. A literature that reflected and expressed the new national reality had its origins in this critical era. Life for nearly everyone, it was hoped, was going to be different, and a new cultural model had to be formed which would make the difference understandable.

By the time of the American 1960s, nearly two hundred years later, Jefferson's "new circumstances" were once more demanding recognition. And the newly elected president, John F. Kennedy, was quoting Jefferson on the need for new words and new phrases to express the making of a new American imagination, for what else could "the transfer of old words to new objects" be?

An American president is more than a national leader, because of the very way our politics work. Like Jefferson before him, John Kennedy himself represented an image of change, and by his election to the Presidency he had become an instructional figure for the new decade. If any persons doubted that the country had shifted course to a different direction, they had only to look to its chief executive, whose projected image and very style suggested a new way of expressing the national cultural model.

Agitation for change by an electorate needs a convenient anchor, and that anchor is most often the style of its political leader, his or her aesthetic image. Planned, specific programs are of greater importance to a nation's changing identity than any one president, but the substance of those programmatic changes can take many decades to achieve. Meanwhile there is the need to advertise one's personality, to define one's style, to marshal support. Therefore image-making, creating one's public self as an almost literary character, becomes profoundly important for the change-directed politician. The study of those images—in aesthetic rather than in simply political terms—must be part of the cultural critic's business. More fre-

3

quently, perhaps, popular decisions are made by a dependence upon those images than by attention to the planks of political platforms which, in their specifics, can be forgotten or even contradicted.

In certain countries the popular will, and the imagination behind it, might be voiced more directly by means of national strikes, special elections, votes of no confidence, or even rioting and civil war. Only once, one hundred years before Kennedy took office, had Americans been thrust into such a crisis. Most other transformations in American life have been codified through regular elections to the Presidency—elections which in their regularlity, orderliness, and concentrated importance have assumed the quality of ritual, for Kennedy a spectacle which was enhanced by the massive electronic media coverage of national politics which had begun in the 1950s and peaked with his electoral campaign. Hence the appealing image of a strikingly unique president was a signal that something new was on the country's mind, whether it was Jeffersonian egalitarianism, Jacksonian democracy, the spirit of Lincoln, or the new social order of Franklin D. Roosevelt.

John Kennedy sought the Presidency with a sense of image equal to that later accorded by the public and historians to these former leaders. What is remarkable is that he had developed this image not after taking his place in history, but during the electoral process. The lofty Age of Jefferson had needed practical Ben Franklin, and Andrew Jackson's style was enhanced by the image of Davy Crockett; even Lincoln had to suffer martyrdom to adequately fill his place in the American imagination. But John Kennedy had presented himself in 1960 as a ready-made symbol of the new America to come, an image all the easier to perceive because it was deliberately juxtaposed to the style of his precedessor, General Dwight D. Eisenhower. "Ice, ice. Our wheels no longer move," Robert Lowell had written at the dawn of Eisenhower's age in 1953:

> Look, the fixed stars, all just alike
> as lack-land atoms, split apart,
> and the Republic summons Ike,
> the mausoleum in her heart.
>
> ("Inauguration Day: January 1953")

In 1960, the image was hot, not cool. Norman Mailer, covering his first political convention, had at once perceived Kennedy in literary rather than political terms; for Mailer, he was a hero. Mailer meant heroism in the classical sense, with Kennedy elevating the entire culture with him. Prefacing his convention commentaries sixteen years (and five presidencies) later, Mailer recalled in *Some Honorable Men* (Boston: Little, Brown & Co.,

1976) just how the national mood and experience were to change, from "summer of 1960, that first of the Kennedy years, in which we became a nation royal with triumphs, tragedies, and ongoing obsessive fears" (p. xii). For it was not merely superficial glamor Kennedy brought with him to the popular image of national leadership. A harsh new light began to show on everything. What Mailer and other informal aestheticians saw as three decades of economic drift in the aftermath of a Depression only sidetracked (and not cured) by world war, and an international deterioriation of politics obscured by domestic demagoguery, were finally to be challenged. And as the economy heated up, so did foreign relations; Americans were earning more, but they also had more to fear. The abstractions of cold war were made suddenly concrete and real, with actual shiploads of Russian missiles steaming toward a possibly catastrophic rendezvous with American forces blockading Cuba. In short, all the abstract and obscure forces of the previous decades were made acutely real to each American—at least to every citizen who could listen to news reports, filed hour by hour, on the possible risks of nuclear war.

John Kennedy's campaign for the Presidency had rested on one consuming political principle increasingly shared by most Americans: that an elected President, and no other single force in American life, could shape and redirect the nation. There is little wonder that Kennedy struck his countrymen as a hero, for that was how Kennedy perceived himself. Nor was Kennedy a hero in a vacuum. The American people were prepared to follow a hero of his style, putting aside the father-protector image of General Eisenhower for the younger, bolder, more innovative style of the war-hero Lieutenant. Apart from his specific programs, and of much greater importance, Kennedy provided a new cultural model: living with crisis, to be experienced as a style of psychodrama. The first new sense apparent in American life during the sixties was that of existing at the extremes. A decade earlier, the threats of international Communism, the hydrogen bomb, and actual warfare in Korea had driven Americans into a psychological retreat; eight years of Eisenhower's administration kept these threats hidden from view behind the cloak of a soporific day-to-day routine. But the U-2 spy-plane incident of 1960 ended this tranquility, and in 1962, when during the Cuban Missile Crisis atomic war became as real a possibility as it has ever been, there was no popular revolt against Kennedy's policy. If anything, the act was received with an atmosphere of high confidence; America had bluffed its opponent, and won. National anxiety, sublimated since the late 1940s, was brought to the surface and purged—the function of a national hero. His own fear for these possibilities had brought the Republican maverick Nelson Rockefeller into the early stages

of the presidential contest in 1960, while the apprehension that world conditions had taken a radical turn kept Democrats away from their party leader
Adlai Stevenson and the policies he had proclaimed in the previous decade.
A sense of urgency, if not ultimacy, pervaded American politics in 1960,
and Kennedy declared himself the man of the hour. The country took him
at his word.

The Kennedy-Nixon face-off of 1960 turned out to be a highly dramatic scene in the theatre of twentieth-century American politics. Only the
succession-breaking elections of Woodrow Wilson (1912), Franklin D.
Roosevelt (1932), and Dwight D. Eisenhower (1952) approached it in terms
of aesthetic drama, and although for 1960 historians claim that the issues
were not as clearly drawn, many voters in retrospect believed they were.
Moreover, Kennedy's tenure in office, climaxed by the tragedy of his
assassination, did even more to convince voters they had made a deliberate
choice between past and future, despite the fact that many of his specific
programs had been stalled in Congress. As Godfrey Hodgson's statistics
from *America in Our Time* (New York: Doubleday, 1976) show, "In
November 1960, one out of every two voters had chosen Kennedy; three
years later, two out of three believed that they had" (p. 5). Richard Nixon
presented a continuity of the old order, both by situation and by preference.
His presidential campaign was built on the image of statesmanship and executive experience. Kennedy, who boasted neither, prevailed by a hair's
breadth in the closest popular vote of the century. Only a tradition-affirm-
ing "dream ticket" of Adlai Stevenson for President and John Kennedy for
Vice-President would have matched Nixon on his cold-war fifties ground,
and this approach the Democratic National Convention firmly rejected.

In 1960 also there were small but noteworthy signs that technology
alone was producing significant changes toward a new age (which would
work to Kennedy's advantage, and to Nixon's disadvantage until he learned
to use them in his 1968 campaign). Airlines had reequipped themselves with
jet transports, cutting transcontinental travel time to a manageable "hop."
Soon direct dialing would make long-distance telephoning as easy as calling
across town. Network news was expanded to a full half-hour in the evening,
equal to the local news, sports, and weather combined, giving audiences the
sense of living in a national community. The country was not only shrinking; it was taking on new dimensions, with little resemblance to the time and
space of even ten years before. Air transportation made it faster and easier
to cover the 1500 miles from Des Moines, Iowa, to New York City than to
travel the 150 highway miles from Spencer, Iowa, to Des Moines. New York
City was suddenly "closer," and in matters such as these the reality of living
in America was changing. Cities deteriorated, suburbs grew. Many Ameri-

cans lived not on their paychecks but on credit, and were issued charge cards in abundance to implement this new way of life. In May 1960, the first oral contraceptives were placed on the market. Publicly and privately, American lives were being reshaped.

The conduct of the 1960 campaign recognized these changes, and Kennedy used them to his advantage. In 1952, relatively few American homes had television sets; by 1960, nearly all of them did, and it was Kennedy's good fortune to play well on TV. In the Kennedy-Nixon debates, for which Nixon used the tactics of a high-school debater, addressing himself to his opponent's issues, Kennedy faced the camera and spoke directly to the nation. And Kennedy's physical image looked so much better on the screen. As Nixon admitted two years later in the writing of *Six Crises* (New York: Doubleday, 1962), "I spent too much time in the last campaign on substance and too little time on appearance; I paid too much attention to what I was going to say and too little to how I would look" (p. 422).

The matter was more than the accidental placement of one politician's photogenic face against another's. The prominence of television coverage and the probing eye of the video camera had changed the way citizens perceived the candidates, and Kennedy was the first to respond to this change. He was both creature and creator of the new reality. Political conventions which formerly pivoted their debates on arcane political matters now rocked to national issues of civil rights, Cuban revolution, and social unrest, for which television viewers had as much concern as the delegates. As the decade concluded, after four assassinations and one near-fatal attempt, national politics had become more than a spectator sport. It was a grisly, life-or-death contest, in which at any moment the candidate might be struck down by a killer, beginning a round-the-clock trauma of national grief and mourning, all properly televised.

Because of his upbringing in the remarkable Kennedy family, John Kennedy had been encouraged to begin forming his own self-image (with an eye to national concerns) long before the campaign of 1960. The boldest statement of this developing image may be found in Kennedy's own *Profiles in Courage,* published by Harper & Row (New York) in 1956. In the Foreword to the book, historian Allan Nevins found it interesting "that so many of Senator Kennedy's instances [of American political courage] show us a parliamentary leader proclaiming his independence of his erring constituency" (p. xi). Kennedy agreed in the Preface that "political courage in the face of constituent pressures" had been his chief interest in coming to write the book, and that his genesis of this theme first came from reading the story of John Quincy Adams, another political heir of a foremost American family, whose image was likewise shaped from childhood.

Defying the pressure of one's constituents was for Kennedy a test of personal integrity and heroism, and so he allowed it to be presented as the theme of the best-seller which would establish his popular image. "When party and officeholder differ as to how the national interest is to be served," he writes early in the book, "we must place the first responsibility we owe not to our party or even to our constituents but to our individual consciences" (p. 15). The essence of democracy is "faith in the wisdom of the people and their views," but Kennedy's ultimate definition of the people in its wisdom is one man facing the issues as an individual, trusting only himself to be right. High elective office then becomes an avenue to personal heroism in the service of national ideals. John Quincy Adams lived by the dictum of his father, that "The magistrate is the servant not of his own desires, not even of the people, but of his God," and Daniel Webster's admonition to his Massachusetts voters was, "I should indeed like to please you; but I prefer to save you, whatever be your attitude toward me." Adams and Webster were Kennedy's men.

The images John Kennedy admired in others were larger than life. His courageous politicians worked the will of God, and withstood mundane claims against their judgment by superior devotion to personal principle of right. The Kennedy hero, then, is Jeffersonian in intellect, Emersonian in spirit, and Jacksonian in personal resolve—an aesthetic image more pertinent to an artistic challenge of the fifties style than to practical politics. Only the Yankee peddler was missing from Kennedy's personal collage of American traits, and mercantile success had been the business of his father's generation. There is even an element of tragedy in his heroes' lives. Speaking of Daniel Webster, Sam Houston, and Thomas Hart Benton, Kennedy recalls "the ignominy of constituent wrath and the humiliation of political downfall at the hands of the states they had loved and championed" (p. 57). But one concept was held in common by all his heroes from Adams, Webster, Benton, and Houston to George Norris and Robert A. Taft: the higher good of the United States above the individual states they represented. That conflict, between union and section, is the tension upon which the Senate is built.

A senator at the time, Kennedy was drawn immediately to the volatile energy which formed the very substance of the Senate, and he used it to make his criterion for greatness. He would approach the presidency the same way, bringing to the surface all the troublesome and rewarding properties his predecessors had kept from view. It was an energy hard to handle, for after the Democratic reign of Roosevelt and Truman, and following the

Republican age of Eisenhower, came a rapid jumble of interrupted presidencies—of Kennedy himself, Johnson, Nixon, and Ford, none of whom was able to occupy the office for as long as tradition, law, and precedent might have allowed.

Kennedy's death, as a cultural shock, has been compared to and linked with the deaths of Ernest Hemingway and Marilyn Monroe, which cultural critics such as Philip Young (*Hemingway: A Reconsideration,* 1966) and Norman Mailer (*Marilyn,* 1973) have studied as aesthetic images of our times. Commentators at the time may have remembered that Kennedy's first words in *Profiles in Courage* evoked Hemingway's definition of the subject, "Grace under pressure," which the author properly acknowledged. Hemingway's moral stance stayed with Kennedy to the book's end, where the question, "What then caused the statesmen mentioned in the preceding pages to act as they did?" was answered in blunt, heroic terms:

> It was not because they "loved the public better than themselves." On the contrary it was precisely because they did *love themselves*—because each one's need to maintain his own respect for himself was more important to him than his popularity with others—because his desire to win or maintain a reputation for integrity and courage was stronger than his desire to maintain his office—because his conscience, his personal standard of ethics, his integrity or morality, call it what you will—was stronger than the pressures of public disapproval—because his faith that *his* course was the best one, and would ultimately be vindicated, outweighted his fear of public reprisal. (pp. 238-239)

Kennedy's success was not as a solitary leader, removed from his people. From his inaugural address through his administration's programs to the risks he took in foreign affairs, his glory was to transform the American people with him, to rise to his call and sustain that fervor after his death. The strength of the momentum he began is evident in the administration of his successor, a quaint and homely man who was destroyed by the sometimes savage quest for glory the younger and more glamorous President had begun. At the time of President Lyndon Johnson's virtual abdication, two political opponents shaped by the Kennedy years—one reflecting the idealism (Eugene McCarthy), the other (Bobby Kennedy) emanating his older brother's fierce determination and reckless daring—stood ready to seize the moment of explosive power their opposition had tried to direct. But the power was too great for either of them, and may even have been too volatile for John Kennedy to handle had he lived, as Norman Mailer would speculate in his fiction.

Virtually all imaginative energy from the 1960s shares its character with the Kennedy legend. Intellectually, he helped create and secure the free intellectual climate so foreign to the previous decade; once begun, this unrestrained political dialogue overran the established channels, and in response to Lyndon Johnson became disruption and dissent. Kennedy's assassination not only built his memory into mythic proportions, but served as further outrage to fuel the decade's protests. But the decisive act was freeing Americans' imaginations and then expanding them, so that alternatives never before dreamed suddenly seemed quite realizable.

Kennedy's image in fiction is no less remarkable. Norman Mailer's *An American Dream* (New York: Dial, 1965) is played off narrator Stephen Rojack's association with Kennedy, and especially with the facets of Rojack's life Kennedy doesn't share (though the real John Kennedy comes close, which is part of the book's teasing effect). It is probable that Kennedy, by accident or circumstance, did not fulfill Mailer's ultimate dream that the President was an incarnation of "the hipster," Mailer's own image of cultural disruption (as detailed in his 1957 essay "The White Negro"). In his 1960 Democratic National Convention coverage, Mailer had suggested Kennedy's promise, that "this candidate for all his record, his good, sound, conventional liberal record has a patina of that other life, the second American life, the long electric night with the fires of neon leading down the highway to the murmur of jazz" (p. 7). Stephen Rojack of *An American Dream* composes a heroic image of his friend Jack Kennedy from the same materials which had entranced America at large: wealth, family name, heroic exploits, and "a vision of treasure, far-off blood, and fear" (p. 1). So that he can have a workable fiction, Mailer transfers these attributes to Deborah Kelly, but the Kennedy connection is obvious: in the novel Rojack meets Deb on a double date with young Congressman Kennedy in 1946, and his ambitions of that night (and their dangers) are worked out in Rojack's subsequent marriage, divorce, act of murder, near-suicide and redemption—as apt a life in the American 1960s as any fictionist is likely to devise.

What is special about Kennedy in this novel is that he and Rojack share a vision of "the abyss," a suspected hollowness at the center of life more final than death, and which can only be resisted by the most daring heroism. Rojack goes on to a career in existential psychology, arguing that "magic, dread, and the perception of death were the roots of motivation" (p. 8). Meanwhile, of course, Kennedy is moving toward the presidency. More than once Rojack relates his own emotions to Kennedy's Cuban missile challenge; that act, we learn, has relieved the previous decade's anxiety and made heroism an easier role to play.

Yet Rojack resists it. After murdering Deborah—a provoked murder,

Mailer would argue—Rojack is tempted to cave in, to let himself be imprisoned instead of fighting for his life. On the other hand, the act of killing has once more touched Rojack with magic; blooded first in the war, he now becomes a domestic savage, living on the edge of his own existence. His and the new decade's future—the young woman Cherry—must be wrested from the underworld figures of night, and Rojack is equal to that challenge, for it is the easy, external one. The tougher battle is with himself.

Rojack's face-off with danger is an excellent metaphor for Kennedy's brand of heroism, which critics at the time derided as heedless daring. To test himself against the abyss he fears, Rojack walks a virtual tightrope around the parapet of a Waldorf balcony apartment. By facing an immediate fear, of his own vertigo in the threat of a very real abyss, Rojack conquers the abyss of metaphor, just as Kennedy's risks during the missile crisis gave the sixties an encouragement to face the coming upheavals and redefinition of values. "There's nothing but magic at the top" (p. 246), Rojack learns, for it is only at the height of human aspirations that we commune with devils and angels.

Mailer's truest portrait of Kennedy, however, is in the realm of metaphor itself. In 1962 Mailer contributed to *Esquire* his single venture in science fiction, which he called "a treatment" (the movie-writer's excuse to deal with pure ideas without the finer trappings of fiction). "The Last Night," as collected in *Cannibals and Christians* (New York: Dial, 1966), is a fantastic portrait of a self-consciously mythical president acting in apocalyptic times—in each case, the style serves as Mailer's approximation of the decade. The dramatic situation is borderline sci-fi, with the planet Earth about to expire from pollution and the president burdened with explaining that a chosen few must be rocketed to another planet to pursue man's future. The president's genius, as was Kennedy's, is to purge guilt by defining purpose; after the directionless years of the 1950s, Kennedy's high-toned statement of purpose changed Americans' images of themselves to match their leader's heroism.

Yet Mailer sees more complexity. Certainly he sees beyond the three short years of Kennedy's Administration to its future consequences as the sixties played out into the seventies. His story introduces a complication which tells the truly awesome and even horrifying nature of such heroic power, for when the only way to launch the embryo spacecraft is to explode the earth itself, the fictional Kennedy does not hesitate. "You would destroy the world for a principle," his wife accuses (p. 389). Mailer's fictional Kennedy survives this charge by transforming the destructive technology into a religion, just as the real president's space program was couched as a spiritual quest (and was so executed by the Bible-quoting astronauts). He redefines the Earth's self-destruction as an act of the phoenix, so that man might find his humanity at last. The president's genius is to bear the full responsibility for this destruction, a burden the real John Kennedy bore every day of his presidency.

The stature of John F. Kennedy, especially his aesthetically created *persona* speaking for a new cultural age, is enhanced by contrasting it to Richard Nixon's. Nixon, of course, was not only Kennedy's opponent in 1960, but in 1968 became the option for people expressing their first organized resistance to the upheavals of sixties culture. The historical circumstance of Richard Nixon makes it possible to isolate and identify the cultural transformations signalled by John Kennedy, for in the 1960 elections Nixon represented the continuity of the old, while in 1968 he styled himself as the candidate opposed to the changes of the past eight years. It was uniquely possible for him to run twice on the same platform, first supporting a continuation of the old order and then asking for a return to it.

Because cultural change was the issue, the platform itself was less important than the advocate's image. Kennedy had determined that the contrast was to be on this level, and Nixon's personal stance was so coincidental with his public image that the contrasts may be fairly drawn. Norman Mailer had seen Kennedy from the very first as a hero, rising above conventional aspirations by explicit trust in his own superior nature. Indeed, Kennedy so dominated the political horizon that his death in 1963 left a vacuum of leadership which Lyndon Johnson could at best only awkwardly fill. Nixon, however, "was the artist who had discovered the laws of vibration in all the frozen congelations of the mediocre," as Norman Mailer put it in *Some Honorable Men* (pp. 424–425). Mailer's invective dates from 1972, and perhaps reflects an elitist scorn, but in even such a lowbrow magazine as *Pageant* (for July 1968) another writer, Hunter S. Thompson, was given space for this diatribe:

> Richard Nixon has never been one of my favorite people, anyway. For years I've regarded his very existence as a monument to all the rancid genes and broken chromosomes that corrupt the possibilities of the American Dream; he was a foul caricature of himself, a man with no soul, no inner convictions, with the integrity of a hyena and the style of a poison toad. The Nixon I remembered was absolutely humorless; I couldn't imagine him laughing at anything except maybe a paraplegic who wanted to vote Democratic but couldn't quite reach the lever on the voting machine. (pp. 6–7)

It is hard to discuss Richard Nixon without becoming pejorative, but that is partly because human inclinations are taught to favor the heroic. When a political figure opposes such heroism, even as a well-reasoned political tactic or as a polemical opposition to such cultural change which elevates heroes in the first place, the image cannot help but be seen as negative.

Where Kennedy's image was expansive, courageous, heroic, and always looking to the larger issue, Nixon set himself as closely played, cautious, ingratiatingly common, and conservative at heart. His *Six Crises,* like Kennedy's *Profiles in Courage,* a study written in repose from public life and with image-making in mind, is a comparable political testament as well, for its subject is again the politician under pressure. The major structural difference is that Kennedy's chapters were drawn from the full range of American history, while Nixon's six episodes were limited to his own political life. But Kennedy was the upward and outward looking hero, always generalizing toward the higher principle, as were the figures in his book. The picture we get of Nixon is as a much more local man.

Nixon's first crisis, he says, was the Alger Hiss case. The issues were potentially as large as any trial Kennedy's courageous heroes had to face: charges of spying, Communist subversion, violation of personal rights, and the investigative propriety of the American Congress. But in *Six Crises* (and presumably in his conduct as well), Richard Nixon viewed his personal challenge as much, much narrower: "This case is going to kill the Committee unless you can prove Chambers' story" (p. 9). As the proportions of the Hiss case grew beyond the interests of the House Un-American Activities Committee, Nixon still gravitated toward the smaller loyalty:

> I must not only do the best I could because of my personal stake in the outcome but also that I must call up an even greater effort to meet the responsibility of representing the institution which had nominated me for office, the Republican Party, as well as fulfilling the hopes of literally thousands of people I would never meet, Republicans and Democrats, who were working for my election and would vote for me. (p. 12)

In matters of controversy, Kennedy's last thoughts were to party and constituency, but for Nixon they came first. The hero of *Six Crises* styles himself as a party man—the very image John Kennedy sought to transcend. The point is that workaday politicians do not deliberately shape new ages, and on this characterization Kennedy and Nixon diverge.

The narrowness is predominant through the next two crises, the 1952 campaign fund scandal (eventually answered by the "Checkers" speech) and Nixon's conduct in the days after President Eisenhower's first heart attack. Nixon's greatest anguish in the former case was that his withdrawal from the ticket might imply his own guilt, and that implication might cost Eisenhower the election, "and I would forever afterwards be blamed for it" (p. 97). Throughout the crisis he remained painfully sensitive to voter reaction, studying it as carefully as Kennedy's heroes wracked their moral consciences. During the heart-attack crisis, Nixon worried less for the General than for his own public image of "getting the best doctors" to Eisenhower's side, even though he admitted the consideration was for mere showmanship, since the most capable doctor had been there from the start. Meanwhile, Nixon is seen carefully measuring his own conduct, so that there might be no suspicion that he was trying to seize power or even fleeting fame.

What most frankly characterizes the image of Nixon, however—and what most starkly contrasts his style with the epoch-maker Kennedy—is his astonishing vulgarity. If Kennedy was the man America chose to express its cultural transformation, Nixon's style was the sure signal for a retreat from that same transformative energy. His fourth and fifth crises were brushes with international Communism. Up through 1962 the keystone of his political career had been resistance to that ideology and political system, and one thinks Nixon would bear some eloquence on the subject. Not so. Years after other statesmen, among them prominent Republicans, had abandoned the myth of monolithic Communism, Nixon could still repeat, "Communism itself is indivisible," both abroad and in America (thereby identifying vaguely liberal tendencies at home with the memory of Joe Stalin's iron fist). Opponents were "Communist thugs," their ideology was "meat for the Communist propaganda grinder," and so forth.

The paucity of Nixon's imagination is reflected in his shallow language. Facing his moment of deepest decision with General Eisenhower, he proclaims, "You've either got to fish or cut bait" as if he is inventing this formulation at the moment of need. His personal thoughts before the Checkers speech, which he knows must be the greatest act of his political life, are, "I looked at my watch and realized that I had only a half-hour left to get cleaned up" (p. 110). Seeking drama in the moment, he describes a tableau: "I turned to Pat and said, 'I just don't think I can go through with this one.' 'Of course you can,' she said." As for the peroration, the part of his speech he knows must clinch victory for his party, he can only blurt, as time runs out, "And remember, folks, Eisenhower is a great man. Folks, he is a great man, and a vote for Eisenhower is a vote for what is good for America" (p. 117).

Nixon's image, and his similar political program—four more years like the last eight—were rejected by voters in favor of Kennedy's animism, both personal and programmatic. But the accidental blandness of 1960, which lost Nixon the Presidency, became the deliberate tactic to help him win in 1968. In that year he saw the highest office was within reach if his campaign could avoid passion and excitement—first to win the Republicans who had enough of that from the disastrous Goldwater candidacy in 1964, and then as an alternative for the American voters, who in the previous twelve months of demonstrations, rioting, assassinations, and military setbacks (the Tet Offensive in Vietnam and Johnson's decision that further escalation was hopeless) might be ready to opt out of the sixties' cultural revolution. Peace Abroad, Peace at Home, and an End to Adventure—in 1968, Richard Nixon had found his place in American politics.

Besides lacking a constructive purpose, Nixon was all too easily depicted as a small, low figure. The ignominious close of the Watergate chapter assured that, but the image sticks only because Nixon lived it for two decades before. Throughout *Six Crises* one finds a man constitutionally unable to see himself as a hero. Hence his challenges are less critical than traumatic, and his advice for facing them is of the self-help, improvement-by-practice variety, just the opposite of Kennedy's sometime Faustian heroics profiled in the annals of the Senate. Adams, Webster, Houston, Benton and the rest challenged the devil. Nixon wriggles against his image in the mirror: "It has been my experience that, more often than not, 'taking a break' is actually an escape from the tough, grinding discipline that is absolutely necessary for superior performance" (p. 105). *Six Crises* is littered with such comments, always coming at the moments of greatest stress where one might expect words to capture a peoples' imagination.

One measure of Nixon's image is the impression he has made on contemporary writers, who have taken his fiction-making capabilities as a head start toward characterization in fully imaginative works of art, as Norman Mailer was able to use the energy of John F. Kennedy in both *An American Dream* and "The Last Night." Robert Coover's *The Public Burning* (New York: Viking, 1977), ostensibly a fabulative replay of the Rosenberg executions in 1953, is in fact a novelistic treatment of Richard Nixon, the book's narrator and true chief character. The contemporaneous action of 1953 is anachronistic, for Coover's Nixon is understandable only in terms of his 1968 and 1972 victories, and in the nature of his 1960, 1962, and especially 1974 defeats. Possessing a political history important enough to rank with the greatest national leaders in history, Coover's Nixon refuses the heroic stereotype in favor of an image which resists all heroism, all change.

Coover's fiction matches up with Nixon's own self-characterization in *Six Crises*. Searching for the imaginative effect (in this case, a consideration of Judge Kaufman's rhetoric in condemning the Rosenbergs), Nixon's language loses all imagination and becomes just a string of slogans: "Would the Reds have dared invade South Korea, rape Czechoslavakia, support the Vietminh and Malayan guerrillas, suppress the freedom-hungry East German workers, if the Rosenbergs had not given them the Bomb?"

But Coover sees Nixon's banality as something more than one man's imaginative insufficiency. Because his position is that of a national leader, both in the fifties and at the end of the sixties, Nixon's cardboard-image sloganeering is an orphic statement of the country's paranoia—that Communism is "The Phantom," threatening everything Americans hold dear. And the threats themselves wash over us like waves of fear and loathing:

> "In 1944," as Congressman Richard Nixon sums it up, "the odds were nine to one in our favor. Today . . . the odds are five to three against us!" And worse to come: in a few short weeks, before the 1949 World Series has even begun, Mao Tse-tung chases Chiang Kai-shek's bony behind off to Formosa and the Reds take over all of China, America is hit by its first postwar recession, the U.S. Secretary of Defense commits suicide, and on top of it all, Russia explodes her first atomic bomb! (p. 14)

The Rosenberg executions are therefore staged as a purgative ritual in Times Square, where the event's theatricality will equal the cheap emotion of the nation's fears:

> V-2s and gas ovens and kamikazes, the hurricane that tore through Overlord, the holocaust at the Coconut Grove, gremlins and goose-steppers, malaria, unfaithful wives, starvation at Guadalcanal, U-boat wolfpacks and Jap snipers and warplanes over Pearl Harbor, vampires and striking workers, hoboes, infantile paralysis, bread lines, bank failures, mortgage foreclosures and dust storms, King Kong and Scarface Al, Wobblies, werewolves, anarchists, Bolsheviks and bootleggers, Filipino guerrillas and Mexican banditos, the Tweed Ring, earth tremors, the Cross of Gold! Down they spiral into irrational panic, as upward swirl the spooks of terrors past! (p. 488)

The elements of Nixon's personality, which stood out in the self-reflections of *Six Crises,* become in Coover's hands the analogs to Nixon's larger national role, that of checking the move toward cultural heroism (Roosevelt and then Kennedy). "I hoped Pat grasped the fact that I was in a major crisis," the fictional Nixon tells us at a key moment, "and was fixing corned beef hash for me with an egg on it." He is antiheroic partly by design, but mostly by default, for he lacks imagination. For much of Coover's book Nixon ponders the Rosenbergs—who they are, how they live, what they mean. "They seemed to live without any structure, without any roots," he decides, "yet they never went anywhere. I'd grown up across the river from the Mexican ghetto of Jim Town, so I knew what one looked like, but I couldn't imagine *living* in a ghetto. I couldn't understand why people didn't just move out and go somewhere else. Lack of imagination or something" (p. 128). Nixon has trouble even thinking of himself beyond the mundane matters of corned-beef hash. "Washington had got the obelisk, Jefferson the dome and circle, Lincoln the cube, what was there left for me?" he ponders. "The pyramid maybe. Something modern and Western would be more appropriate, but all I could think of were the false fronts in the old cowtowns" (p. 265).

Nixon's own politics suggest that Coover's theory of the man as a ritualist fits history as well. Nixon's election in 1968 was ritualistic on the part of the voters, and his reelection campaign four years later stressed this element all the more. But it was a ritual meant to close the American 1960s, to signal an end to the decade's growth and disruptions. Once that service was performed, the Nixon Administration became an empty, parodistic shell, fully incapable of real government and leading instead to the paranoic abuses revealed in Watergate. New styles of journalism—including the investigative reporting of Robert Woodward and Carl Bernstein in *All the President's Men* and *The Final Days,* the innovative techniques of Hunter S. Thompson, and even the confessional self-analyses of John Dean in *Blind Ambition*—would document just how ineffective the last Nixon Administration was, despite its highly publicized diplomatic dealings (themselves to be criticized later in the attacks upon Henry Kissinger).

Literary portraits themselves have changed. While he was still effective in his public image as the decade-ender, Philip Roth's Nixon could only be seen as the object of rude, embarrassing jokes (as in Roth's *Our Gang,* written in 1969 and 1970). But once Kent State and then Watergate made the closing of the sixties a moot point, characterizations such as Coover's could emerge to show Nixon's image for what it was, beyond all the petty insults and cheap shots the critics might take.

The quality of life lived in the American 1970s—enhanced personal freedom, candor and accountability of government, a whole new sense of priorities and values—is attributable in part to the imaginative breakthoughs of the sixties. One glance at their absence in the 1950s seals the case, though the prominence of new cultural styles in the seventies is a clue to the causal nature of this change, despite the many elements of reaction. Though the activism of the sixties died with the shock of Kent State, many of the more personal counterculture values were adopted into mainstream American life. The most visible effects, from the fashionability of high-priced drugs to the more seriously entertained alternatives to conventional marriage, have proven disconcerting to some commentators.

At this writing the American 1970s are being rung out by critic Tom Wolfe as "the Me Decade," a period of hedonistic self-indulgence repugnant in its decadence. Literary critics such as John Gardner (*On Moral Fiction,* 1978) and Gerald Graff (*Literature Against Itself,* 1979) have taken Wolfe's diagnosis of cultural solipsism and applied it to both the innovative fiction and deconstructionist criticism dominant since the sixties. But beneath this surface so disagreeable to conservative eyes may be found substantial changes in the day-to-day manner people live their lives, far beyond the titillations of a ménage in the bedroom, cocaine in the sugar bowl, or Jacques Derrida on the bookshelf.

In *New Age Blues* (New York: Dutton, 1979) Michael Rossman voices his own more substantial fears for the seventies as they develop into the eighties. He admits that the displacement of traditions in the sixties brought the counterculture close to what he considers benign chaos, where true nonauthoritarian learning ("the ability to create for oneself new frames to inhabit from the material available") might have sustained itself into the seventies. But instead the movement panicked in "the existential amazement of being at the Edge, where reality breaks open into the Chaos before it is reformed." This panic, Rossman believes, has influenced the Human Potential movement from which Tom Wolfe derives his "Me Decade" epitaph:

> The intense questioning and disruption of social reality, and the wave of experiments in reconstituting its processes and institutions that marked the 1960s, had prepared and in fair degree demanded a complementary mass questioning and re-exploration of private being and consciousness—for when the fabric of society is torn and reconfigured, so is that of the self, the two being so nearly one. (p. xi)

The nature of this personal-growth-and-consciousness movement is schizophrenic, Rossman says, because its emphasis of the individual has been vitiated by a contradictory reliance upon authority, especially the dictatorial fascination exercised by such guru-leaders as Werner Erhard, Arthur Janov, and Richard Alpert/Ram Dass who quiet personal fears of the abyss by offering a tried and true master's way. Rossman's worry for the eighties is that today's security blanket will become tomorrow's totalitarianism. Hence the complementary powers of a new heroism enhanced by personal freedom which emerged from the sixties have been by no means free of controversy.

One thesis which is rarely questioned, however, is that the genesis of these new powers can be traced to the Kennedy excitement of the early 1960s. Looking backward from the eighties, so many subsequent cultural happenings can be traced to that apparently boundless enthusiasm. The Kennedy legend has survived its scandalous debunking in the seventies, its discrediting in the matter of foreign policy (the Bay of Pigs fiasco, for example), and the violent student protests of the President's own decade. Covering the Berkeley Free Speech movement for *The Nation* magazine (September 27, 1965), the ubiquitous Hunter Thompson noted that "Student radicals today may call Kennedy a phony liberal and a glamorous sellout, but only the very young will deny that it was Kennedy who got them excited enough to want to change the American reality, instead of just quitting it" (p. 155). It was the Beat generation of the fifties, Thompson reminded his readers, who had simply dropped out.

Still, political campaigns are recorded for the most part by working journalists and then analyzed by conventional historians, despite the fact that the best politicians (and the worst) are in fact masters of fiction. Fiction itself, the territory of man's imagination, may offer a better picture of the Kennedy spirit, especially when the characters are protopoliticians themselves. Two novels published during the first years of the Kennedy administration, *One Flew Over the Cuckoo's Nest* and *Catch-22,* caught the spirit of the decade as clearly as John Kennedy enunciated it, and it is in their new styles of heroism and personal freedom that the image of things to come may be found.

CHAPTER TWO

McMurphy and Yossarian
as Politicians

Randall Patrick McMurphy, the small-time gambler and brawler who seeks relief from prison work-farm drudgery by bluffing his way into a mental asylum, and Captain Yossarian, an Air Corps bombardier who thinks people (such as German gunners) are trying to kill him, are political forces within their own novels. McMurphy leads an open rebellion against the ward's authoritarian head nurse, and Yossarian debates conventional notions of authority, and even rational order, in war. Beyond their personal revolts, each argues for a new order of reality, whether it be in rejecting the plans for the mental and social hygiene an institutional state would impose, or speaking out against the routine absurdity which through bureaucratic administration can come to pass as fact.

Both McMurphy and Yossarian become politicians in a larger sense, as culture heroes for the bold new decade of the American 1960s. Their creators, Ken Kesey and Joseph Heller, wrote outside of the literary establishment, and neither pursued the usual course of a "developing" author. *One Flew Over the Cuckoo's Nest* (New York: Viking, 1962) and *Catch-22* (New York: Simon and Schuster, 1961) are uniquely solitary works, far better known than their authors, and each serving as a talisman to the new culture. Standing alone because they anticipated (rather than continued) a tradition, they became known as underground novels, popularized and propagated by word-of-mouth recommendations quite independent of the establishment reviews and best-seller lists which continued to reflect the more closely drawn manners and morals (consider Saul Bellow, Bernard Malamud, John Updike) of the fifties. McMurphy and Yossarian were the first underground literary heroes of the new activist generation, proclaiming revolutionary new values which were as clear a signal as Kennedy's election that a new style and possibly a new reality were imminent.

One Flew Over the Cuckoo's Nest and *Catch-22* were first of all campus novels, and by the early 1960s academic conditions were such that a new market was available to insinuate these books into the consciousness of the youth culture, without using the traditional systems of distribution more likely to remain in conservative hands. The boom in higher education produced large classes of freshmen and sophomores, taught by a growing cadre

20

of graduate assistants, and these books became two of the most widely taught novels in such circumstances. A decade earlier English classes were just discovering the great modernist works of the 1920s; but as the sixties dawned, literature suddenly became a pressing contemporary concern. Kesey and Heller spoke directly to young collegians, in terms they soon would echo in their own protests against society. McMurphy and Yossarian were initially presented as heroes by a young, newly (and even prematurely) enfranchised group of teachers as the first chosen models in a new educational situation. Such coincidence and reinforcement between methods and materials is one of the many reasons why the sixties, as a decade of change, made such an immediate impact.

One Flew Over the Cuckoo's Nest speaks in the present tense, a signal of currency and of performance. The book *happens* like a movie. And it speaks directly to the reader, trusting the quality of *voice* to carry its effect far beyond the limited nature of its theme. "Who's the bull goose loony here?" shouts McMurphy as he bursts into the closely played world of the mental ward, its conformity and repression a perfect image of the fifties. What Mac says is important, but how he says it is what matters, embellishing his very presence with an aura of performance allusive to the wildness in America's past and the promise of her future:

> "Then you tell Bull Goose Harding [the effeminate spokesman for the inmates] that R. P. McMurphy is waiting to see him and that this hospital ain't big enough for the two of us. I'm accustomed to being top man. I been a bull goose catskinner for every gyppo logging operation in the Northwest and bull goose gambler all the way from Korea, was even a bull goose pea weeder on that pea farm at Pendleton—so I figure if I'm bound to be a loony, then I'm bound to be a stompdown dadgum good one. Tell this Harding that he either meets me man to man or he's a yaller skunk and better be outta town by sunset." (p. 19)

The inmates realize at once that he is a politician, even a mythic one, incorporating aspects of the car salesman, stock auctioneer, and sideshow pitchman. McMurphy hits the ward like a bolt of summer lightning, not just for what he is in himself, but for what needs to be done in the hospital.

The hospital Mac has faked his way into is like none other in American fact or fiction. Phone wires whistle in the walls, electric current roars through conduits to appliances, fog machines deliberately obscure the grounds, and nuts-and-bolts technicians pull spare parts in and out of the patients at will. These images are metaphorical, at least to the reader. But to the novel's narrator, a Columbia River Indian named "Chief Broom"

Bromden, they are strikingly real. Although officially described as a mental case, the Chief in fact suffers from (or enjoys the benefit of) a rich visual imagination. What may only be subtle intention on the part of the head nurse becomes in Bromden's mind a startling, physical actuality, and her manner of ward discipline is not only expressed by him in fantastic mechanical terms, but is extended to a larger vision of society, entirely restructured according to the nurse's ideal of absolute, repressive order.

Chief Bromden's mind resists the nurse's plan, and by playing deaf and dumb he is able to overhear what the other inmates miss. What the fifties called a disability, the sixties would redefine as great and touching eloquence. But his imagination has an even more important role in this novel. It is the fertile field on which McMurphy's ideas fall, the sensitive screen against which his flamboyant actions are played. If the Chief has expressed the imaginative truth of the nurse's repressive manner, he is also the one to mythologize McMurphy's resistance and rebellion. A hero such as Mac needs first of all to be perceived as a hero; and as our eyes and ears in this novel, the conventionally mute Chief Bromden becomes the expression of McMurphy's greatness.

A limited and closely defined set of images fills Chief Bromden's mind: the action among the ward's inmates, the Big Nurse's regimentation and more subtle manipulation of those inmates, the foreboding institutional and technological atmosphere (described as "operations of the Combine"), and McMurphy's posture in opposition to it all. Mac is more vitally healthy than the pallid, insipid patients, for his own life of self-assertion is in direct contrast to the passive, depressive, and victimized stance inmates like Harding and Bibbit have taken toward the world. Because he has led the footloose life of a drifter, Mac has remained untouched by the Combine, which would use marriage and responsibility as pressures molding potential individuals into suburban ciphers, one interchangeable with another. *One Flew Over the Cuckoo's Nest* was one of the first novels to deal imaginatively with the hidden persuaders, the organization men, the lonely crowd, and other current sociological images of the fifties for a world of plenty the sixties generation would not worship but fear. Very shortly the age of affluence would be condemned as spiritually impoverished. The popularity of Chief Bromden's fears about the Combine is among the first signs of a change in cultural sentiment:

> The ward is a factory for the Combine. It's for fixing up mistakes made in the neighborhoods and in the schools and in the churches, the hospital is. When a completed product goes back out into society, all fixed up good as new, *better* than new sometimes, it brings joy to the Big Nurse's heart; something that came in all twisted different is now a

> functioning, adjusted component, a credit to the whole outfit and a
> marvel to behold. Watch him sliding across the land with a welded grin,
> fitting into some nice little neighborhood where they're just now dig-
> ging trenches along the street to lay pipes for city water. He's happy
> with it. He's adjusted to surroundings finally. . . . (p. 38)

In the 1950s social conformity had been the ideal for material progress, and
in the forties it was an even loftier virtue as part of the war effort. The new
culture in the sixties questioned both, and Kesey emphasizes the fatal nature
of "the Combine" by making its principal victim the Vanishing American
who narrates this novel, a man who is being psychically destroyed by the
same forces of social progress that killed his tribe.

Against these social forces, which by the 1960s had come to be perceived as threats, McMurphy places himself as a revolutionary hero. He is
first of all a disruptionist, against the Big Nurse in particular and authority
in general, and especially against the type of authority that inhibits self-ex-
pression and places limits on the individual. Like disruptionists of the coming decade, he sees that most of his acts must be theatrical, and much of his
early effort is spent in gaming and baiting the Big Nurse. He challenges
votes at her group meetings, smears her nurse's station window, disrupts
her ward routine—all staged to the pleasure of the observing inmates. Even
the pettiest acts are deliberately symbolic. They weaken the nurse, but more
importantly they strengthen the men. Randall Patrick McMurphy is the first
fictional hero to practice that key strategy of sixties leadership: *raising the
consciousness of the people.* The ward inmates represent a cross section of
American society, but his most responsive pupil is Chief Broom, a Native
American, the First American, whom the progress of events has reduced to
a deathlike silence. McMurphy restores the Chief to life, "blows him up
whole again," and so reanimates America—just what the culturally regen-
erative movements of the sixties sought to do.

McMurphy's role as animator is worth looking at more closely.
Although the ward he checks into is physically and emotionally lifeless, its
spirit broken by the strictures of the Big Nurse, McMurphy does not try to
change any of its essential characteristics. Rather he transforms it into
something positive. He does not deny that he and the others are "loonies,"
but rather asserts his looniness as part of the mechanics of greatness; he will
become "bull goose loony" and offers the same potential to anyone else.
Mad is beautiful, McMurphy preaches to these self-defeated patients who
have let society's label destroy them. The therapies Mac develops do not
contradict the inmates' condition, but rather exploit their so-called
disabilities in order to create a new source of strength. One of the happiest
moments in the ward (and one of the most enjoyably readable sections of

the novel) is an interlude when the whole crew plays Monopoly, replete with bizarre rules and hallucinated playing pieces conceivable only in a madhouse. The equally improbable fishing trip lets every man play his own role to the fullest. McMurphy is truly a transformative hero. He changes the terms under which they are living, rather than changing their lives themselves. Laughter is his great weapon—"that big wide-open laugh of his. Dials twitch in the control panel at the sound of it" (p. 17). It is the one thing an otherwise totally helpless person can do, McMurphy teaches the men. And Chief Bromden remembers it as a weapon his father and other tribesmen used against the government. Though laughter is a physical expression, its substance is intellectual, even imaginative. In this way McMurphy is advocating a proletarian revolution of the mind; it is his new valuation of the terms of life which makes him a threat to the establishment. McMurphy is inventing a new way of perceiving reality, which is nothing less than a new reality itself.

The radical nature of McMurphy's challenge to the establishment is shown by the way the establishment strikes back. Emotional castration has kept the lesser inmates in line, but Mac's challenge has come from his imagination, and so castration of his mind—lobotomy—is the nurse's ultimate response. "I guess if she can't cut below the belt she'll do it above the eyes," Mac tells the Chief. For his part, Mac stays with the group and sacrifices himself for it—a new style of American heroism. The heroic tradition had been for a Natty Bumppo to strike off on his own, or for a Captain Ahab to sacrifice the group for his own ideal. "Anointest my head with conductant," Mac tells the electroshock therapist who begins his crucifixion, "Do I get a crown of thorns?" The Chief remarks several times how McMurphy has been weakened by his quest. As the men increase, Mac decreases, until by the end, when the inmates have taken control of their lives and the Chief has performed his superhuman act of throwing a hydrotherapy fount through the window and taking off for freedom, he is completely effaced from the novel. But only in body. The men walk with his swagger, boast with his bravado. McMurphy was the restorative spirit, and they have been restored.

One Flew Over the Cuckoo's Nest presents a transformed vision of reality as well. And not just because the book's narrator has a richly imaginative way of perceiving things. Rather, that narrator has the special ability to play with the technical givens of his situation. He doesn't suffer from the mechanization of the Big Nurse's world; instead, he incorporates all its facets as elements of imaginative play, in a game he—not the nurse— controls. Even routine exposition benefits from this trick, making a richer, more imaginative, and ironically more personalized world to live in. "A tall bony old guy, dangling from a wire screwed in between his shoulder blades, met McMurphy and me at the door when the aides brought us in," the Chief narrates. "He looked us over with yellow, scaled eyes and shook his head. 'I wash my hands of the whole deal,' he told one of the colored aides, and the wire drug him off down the hall" (p. 264). The first characterization of the Big Nurse herself has been similarly composed of such native elements as the Chief finds handy for the art he can make from his world: "She slides through the door with a gust of cold and locks the door behind her and I see her fingers trail across the polished steel—tip of each finger the same color as her lips. Funny orange. Like the tip of a soldering iron." Throughout the novel Chief Bromden plays with his made-up images, his junk-sculpture from the manic-depressive ward. The nurse leaves a lipstick stain on a coffee cup, but the Chief believes "That color on the rim of the cup must be from heat, touch of her lips set it smoldering." The importance of the Chief's technique is obvious when we see the other typical activity of his mind: reconstructing idyllic memories of his young manhood on the Columbia River, before the government dispossessed his tribe. Both procedures are vital to his psychic health, as he refreshes himself in happy memories and actively works on the present to create a life of fiction. As the sixties developed, thinkers as various as psychiatrist R. D. Laing and philosopher Norman O. Brown would propose the same therapy to the culture at large.

But foremost is the way McMurphy, and especially the idea of McMurphy, operates on Chief Bromden's mind. Mac fills the Indian's imagination as the hero needed to revive him—"The iron in his boot heels crackled lightning out of the tile. He was the logger again, the swaggering gambler, the big redheaded Irishman, the cowboy out of the TV set walking down the middle of the street to meet a dare" (p. 189). As he has played with the mechanical image of the nurse, Chief Bromden embellishes the person of Randall McMurphy until it represents nearly every hero America has known for her mythic sustenance. For what he must do, McMurphy is made larger than life, too large even to be believable, just as the Chief's narration is too poetic to pass for day-to-day speech. "I been silent so long now," he tells us, "it's gonna roar out of me like floodwaters and you think the guy telling this is ranting and raving my *God;* you think this is too horrible to have really happened, this is too awful to be the truth!" (p. 8). Cultural conditions at the turn of the sixties demanded a prophet. "It's still hard for me to have a clear mind thinking on it," the Chief admits. "But it's the truth even if it didn't happen."

Kesey's novel invents a new reality by means of voice, especially voice expressing an imaginatively new construction of the world. Joseph Heller's *Catch-22* reaches deeper for its reconstruction. Although the novel does have a surface action, with characters and themes drawn from World War II, its real substance is language, especially the grammar and syntax which philosophers tell us intimate the deep structure of reality. Such criticism began in America with Noam Chomsky's studies of transformational grammar in 1957, and structuralism as a method became popular here only in the 1960s. But even for subject matter, one can't forget that Heller's picture of World War II eclipses conventional realism. For one, it comes nearly two decades after the event, after the country had been through Korea and was gearing up for Vietnam. In 1961, hardly anybody was writing realistic fiction about World War II, and the author of *Catch-22* was not about to begin.

Instead, Heller's purpose was larger: he was redefining World War II as a way of revising our notions of what passes for reality. And at the very first came a new grammar to reflect this orientation. "The Texan turned out to be good-natured, generous and likeable," we are told early on. "In three days nobody could stand him." Everything that comes up for discussion is handled in this fractured rhetoric. "Colonel Cargill, General Peckem's troubleshooter, was a forceful, ruddy man," we are told. "Before the war he had been an alert, hard-hitting, aggressive marketing executive. He was a very bad marketing executive. Colonel Cargill was so awful a marketing executive that his services were much sought after by firms eager to establish losses for tax purposes" (p. 27). Heller continues at paragraph length with such descriptions, and it turns out there are very real (if financially innovative) reasons for Cargill's success. But they are expressed in a total butchery of conventional syntax and reason—"He had to start at the top and work his way down," "He was a self-made man who owed his lack of success to nobody," and so on. Heller is not only inventing a new way to perceive reality; he is inventing a new reality, based on a reversal of values carried over from the earlier world view. The big surprise is that most everyone assumed that earlier world view still prevailed.

The military provides a perfect setting for the logical proof of such an illogical re-creation of reality, and is an example accessible to most Americans. Being in the Army, or just watching it operate, gives one the impression that this is a colossal ship of fools, an absurdist enterprise made operational only by its vaguely assumed importance of mission. *Catch-22* makes fun of Army bureaucracy, Army logic, and Army inefficiency. But it also makes a deeper impression than the many popular entertainments of the time, such as Mac Hyman's *No Time for Sergeants,* Phil Silver's *Sgt.*

Bilko/You'll Never Get Rich television series, and their imitators. Like Kesey, Joseph Heller enjoys playing with the imaginative possibilities of off-kilter situations, and his virtuosity with language creates an enjoyable, verbally artistic picture:

> The colonel dwelt in a vortex of specialists who were still specializing in trying to determine what was troubling him. They hurled lights into his eyes to see if he could see, rammed needles into nerves to hear if he could feel. There was a urologist for his urine, a lymphologist for his lymph, an endrocrinologist for his endocrines, a psychologist for his psyche, a dermatologist for his derma; there was a pathologist for his pathos, a cystologist for his cysts, and a bald and pedantic cetologist from the zoology department at Harvard who had been shanghaied ruthlessly into the Medical Corps by a faulty anode in an I.B.M. machine and spent his sessions with the dying colonel trying to discuss *Moby Dick* with him. (p. 15)

From the silliness of "isms" and "ists," which pervades modern life far beyond the Army, Heller has extended and embellished the situation, from the reasonableness of "urologist/urine" to the craziness of "pathologist/pathos." The root of his method is the faulty syllogism, the unequal equation that urologist is to urine as pathologist is to pathos, but such wacky structures are revealed as the principles on which a new reality has been built. If a Harvard cetologist can get drafted into the Medical Corps, how less ridiculous is it for him to discuss Melville with his patients? In this way Heller's novel defines and clarifies a new reality we might not otherwise believe was there.

Needless to say, American novels did not provide such phenomenological service in the 1950s. But neither does Heller go the way of the French *nouveau roman,* for he animates *Catch-22* with the behavior of living human beings whose deep and interesting personalities must respond to the phenomenological surface so described. Yossarian is the foremost example. He is the one combatant who suffers from the otherwise paranoid fears, that "they are trying to kill me," which only the transformed reality of World War II makes real. Because of his ultimate reasonability in the face of compounded absurdity, Yossarian is the one to challenge the orders which systematically increase the number of combat missions to be flown before the men can complete them. But his personal life shows that he is, just as much as anyone, involved in the new reality. He particpates in it, as parody, by censoring letters with a bored irrationality equal to anything his commanders might force upon him. To break the monotony, he invents syntactic games. One day he censors all modifiers, the next adverbs. "The next day he made war on articles. He reached a much higher plane of creativity the following day when he blacked out everything in the letters but *a, an* and *the*. That erected more dynamic intralinear tensions, he felt, and in just about every case left a message far more universal'' (p. 8). He signs his name ''Washington Irving,'' later ''Irving Washington,'' planting the seeds for a CID investigation only a bit less Byzantine than the novel's action itself.

Yossarian plays with sentences, but Heller uses *Catch-22* to show that our own sentences have placed us in structures we cannot fulfill, such as Colonel Cathcart's hopeless situation, completely self-created and expressed to himself in terms of a grammatical ideal: ''He could measure his own progress only in relation to others, and his idea of excellence was to do something at least as well as all the men his own age who were doing the same thing even better'' (p. 185). Other roles are fulfilled all too well. Milo Minderbinder develops a trading syndicate equal to any of the large corporations which asserted their supremacy after World War II, and his method is located in the same bizarre language structures:

> ''I make a profit of three and a quarter cents an egg by selling them for four and a quarter cents an egg to the people in Malta I buy them from for seven cents an egg. Of course, *I* don't make the profit. The syndicate makes the profit. And everybody has a share.'' (p. 226)

His M & M Enterprises stands simply for Milo Minderbinder, with the ''&'' added ''to nullify the impression that the syndicate was a one-man operation.'' Milo can no more eliminate the middleman in his operation (himself) than the nurses can eliminate the middleman in the case of the head-to-toe-bandaged soldier in white, where each morning a bottle of intravenous fluid is plugged in and a bottle of urine taken away. To eliminate the middleman would be to eliminate the soldier himself. Like the ''&'' in Milo's enterprises, he is the necessary grammatical structure needed to make this mad world work. To show the totally arbitrary nature of war, Milo contracts bomb runs for the Germans, taking on bridges, emplacements, and finally his own airfield. And he is right: the technique is more efficient. For tactical warfare, at least, the middleman has been eliminated.

Yossarian is a restorative hero because he wants to wake up those around him to the hideous facts the Army's new reality is obscuring:

> ''They're trying to kill me,'' Yossarian told him calmly.
> ''No one's trying to kill you,'' Clevinger cried.
> ''Then why are they shooting at me?'' Yossarian asked.
> ''They're shooting at *everyone,*'' Clevinger answered. ''They're trying to kill everyone.''
> ''And what difference does that make?'' (p. 16)

He is an expert at fending off the Army's perverse logic. He refuses to fly more missions. When the Colonel asks him what would happen if everyone acted that way, Yossarian replies that then he'd be an even greater fool to act differently.

Yossarian discovers a deeper reality beneath the Army's new provisions. The Colonel's self-aggrandizement and Milo's mania for capitalism convince him that there is a more substantial goal than bombing Germans. The war, in fact, is a game board on which senior officers battle to seize each other's power, and the real progress of the war is the advancement of their own careers. General Peckem of Special Services develops a master plan to incorporate all of the Air Corps units into his own, only to be subverted by Colonel Scheisskopf, whose solitary aim is to assemble more and more men to march for him. Some tactics developed in World War II work much better against the other generals than against the Germans. In Heller's own time, a war was being fought in Vietnam which yielded none of the traditional military goals, but which amply satisfied militaristic needs: a corps of senior officers, stalled in rank by the vicissitudes of a peacetime Army, were given the combat commands they needed for proper career advancement. Major Josiah Bunting's novel *The Lionheads* (1972) drew the same conclusion from actual Vietnam command experience, but Heller's *Catch-22* sensed these conditions in American culture in 1961, just as the Vietnam war began.

The repetitious, cumulative structure of *Catch-22* reflects the nonlinear form of Heller's new reality. Nothing develops in clear succession, nothing advances in a clear line. Rather, scenes are repeated over and over again, each time coming into sharper focus, until at the end the reader is overwhelmed by an event, anticipated several times in *déjà vu* so that all its elements carry twice or even ten times the strength they might normally have. The death of Snowden is the clearest case. Its cumulative repetition controls the mood of the whole novel, which gradually shifts from hilarity to horror. Time and space are reconstituted as elements of reality, simply because they are experienced differently in the world of *Catch-22*.

Aspects of military bureaucracy also contribute to a reshaped nature of the real. The "dead soldier in Yossarian's tent" is a problem because he took off on a mission, and died on it, before the duty officer could check him in. Since the command does not officially know that he "lived," it cannot report his death. When Hungry Joe's light plane crashes into a mountainside, Doc Daneeka is declared dead, a victim of the opposite situation: he had added his name to the flight manifest as an easy way to earn flight pay. Yossarian receives a medal for fouling up a bomb run, since the Colonel can think of no other way to cover the embarrassment. And so on, to the point of debasing all values of life and death, courage and cowardice, heroics and dishonor.

To be effective, America must fashion a new definition of heroism. This was the conclusion social philosophers and even natural scientists came to as the decade ended. The Promethean hero who provided a model to expand and develop the country was no longer adequate to a world of depleted resources and diminished environment. Notions of success and failure had to be readjusted; the new hero became Protean, as described by Joseph Meeker (*The Comedy of Survival,* 1974), Paul Shepard (*The Tender Carnivore and the Sacred Game,* 1973), Loree Rackstraw (*Earth Mother and Father Time,* in progress), and others. Curiously, Heller was able to find an image for this new heroism within World War II. "You put too much stock in *winning wars,*" the old Italian man talls Nately. He explains that "The real trick lies in *losing wars,* in knowing which wars can be *lost.* Italy has been losing wars for centuries, and just see how splendidly we've done nonetheless." France wins and languishes; Germany loses and prospers. "Italy won a war in Ethiopia and promptly stumbled into serious trouble. Victory gave us such insane delusions of grandeur"—the Prometheus complex, Rackstraw and her colleagues would later suggest—"that we helped start a world war we hadn't a chance of winning. But now that we are losing again, everything has taken a turn for the better, and we will certainly come out on top again if we succeed in being defeated" (p. 240).

The old man's logic takes the same form as all *Catch-22* rhetoric. Its strategy of systematic reversal underscores the point that a new reality, quite the opposite of the old, has taken hold; the screwed-up action of the Army only represents an undirected foundering among these new currents. Heller's point has not been just to mimic and ridicule the chaos encountered with the coming of such a new world, but rather to clarify the changes in values so that life may be lived with more happiness and success. "Anything worth living for is worth dying for," Nately argues. But the old Italian corrects him and puts him back on course. "And anything worth dying for," he tells the young soldier, "is certainly worth living for."

Although it never appeared on a best-seller list, *Catch-22* became an underground classic in the 1960s, selling over six million copies, more than twice the cumulative sales of 1961's top listed novel, *The Agony and the Ecstasy.* The only serious novel to outsell it, in fact, has been *One Flew Over the Cuckoo's Nest,* according to figures published in *The Wilson Quarterly* (Winter 1978). To find better-selling fiction, one must go to the pulp masterpieces of Jacqueline Susann, Erich Segal, and Richard Bach. And even there the margin above *Catch-22* is less than 15 percent.

In a country as commercialized as the United States, it is difficult to identify authentic popular culture within the products of mass-media entertainment, and even harder to single out legitimate cultural trends. For novels, one way is to see if phrases and attitudes work their way out of the books and into the popular ambience of the times. Kesey's novel does this in reverse: it builds itself out of elements widely available (and operative) in the popular culture, from the multiform images of McMurphy to the mythic stature of its narrator, the Indian, Chief Bromden. But *Catch-22* was a more formative novel. Ostensibly about World War II, it described that conflict in terms which were to become innovatively accurate for a war just beginning in Vietnam, a war which defied all previous stereotypes and which could be discussed coherently only in the wacky new grammar Heller's novel had invented. "Catch-22" became a code word for any self-contradicting bureaucratic order in society, used by people who never read the novel. And the qualities of Yossarian became a new heroic image for the decade, a new image for the male star, whether for Dustin Hoffman playing in *The Graduate,* Robert Blake in *Electra-Glide in Blue,* or Alan Arkin playing Yossarian himself in Mike Nichols' film of *Catch-22*

That movie audiences did not see adaptations of *One Flew Over the Cuckoo's Nest* and *Catch-22* until after the decade ended is even better proof that, as novels, they existed outside the pressure of commercial entertainment. If a book is successful as an economic investment, the film version usually comes a year later. Advertising, paperback publication, and film distribution reinforce each other in "tie-ins," and the product is marketed like an LP record—or, better yet, like a line of frozen pizzas. Under such conditions it is hard to tell whether the American public is responding to a deeply felt image in its developing culture, or whether it is being sold a bill of goods.

The movies from Kesey's and Heller's novels came much later, in the early 1970s. In their case a complementary principle of the American film industry was employed: if some films are made in response to commercial success, others try to manufacture a commercial success out of something already existing in the popular culture. Here the people supply the product to the industry, instead of the other way around. For nearly ten years McMurphy and Yossarian had helped express the redirection of a culture. They were popular far beyond the already large sales of their novels; their attitudes and beliefs pervaded American life, so that by the later 1960s they marched in the streets to protest similar institutional and bureaucratic monstrosities perpetrated by some who commanded our government. Davy Crockett, Daniel Boone, Paul Bunyan, and other such representative

American characters were not created by a commercial entertainment complex, but their authentic popularity made them apt materials for commercial use. McMurphy and Yossarian described the new reality which underlay the politics of the 1960s, and the extent of their popularity, in their respective novels and films, flanks that decade almost as neatly as the numerological way we count off decades themselves.

CHAPTER THREE

Frank O'Hara and Richard Brautigan: Personal Poetry

Of all the arts in the 1960s, poetry made the most abrupt about-face. In the previous decade other forms of expression—painting and music especially—were showing signs of advance, but the writing of poetry was a closed profession, not even opening its sentiments to those who read it:

> poetry was declining
> Painting advancing
> we were complaining
> it was '50.

When Frank O'Hara wrote those lines, he was doubtlessly thinking of the modernist poetry which still held sway, bowing only to its academic extension in the hands of professor-poets who had a vested interest in teaching it. The great works of T. S. Eliot, Wallace Stevens, and e. e. cummings which were written as much as half a century before had a petrifying effect on the present. Their modernism had defined the new era's first compelling image of itself, and even forty years later it was as difficult to recast that image as to dislodge Einstein from his position of preeminence in modern physics. The second generation of modernists were even more of an obstacle. The intellectual denseness of a Robert Lowell or an Allen Tate produced a confessional poetry which served to alienate and a lyricism which spoke more of the poet's distance from his readership than proximity. The poet was a superior, obscure, and sometimes cold person, and poetry of the time reflected this temperament.

In the 1960s this image was replaced by its striking opposite. Through the popularization of Rod McKuen and Leonard Cohen poetry had become a mass-market product, and the personality of the poet, even in styles far above the easy sentimentality of these two new writers, was drastically affected. The poet, in sixties' ambience, was now someone who spoke directly to the people, even conversationally. Poetic discourse was speech which unified and identified, not separated and stratified. Poetic sentiment implied the sharing of feelings; in the case of Cohen and especially McKuen, this sentiment was often base and common itself, but such slightness of substance was a desired counter tactic to the smug and serious mood of the fifties.

Such nonexclusive lyricism became the hallmark of sixties poetry. Cohen and McKuen were the extreme of its popularization. If their sentimentality often seemed of the greeting-card variety (and their lines sometimes did appear in a new form of poster art marketed in card shops), it was because the poet was now expected to speak directly to the people and their everyday concerns. Leonard Cohen and Rod McKuen became projected self-images just as much as the popular singers of the day—in fact, both of them became successful musical performers of their own works. Leonard Cohen and Bob Dylan could be fruitfully compared, even by the same standards, in a way that T. S. Eliot and Perry Como could never be.

A major ingredient in the work of both Frank O'Hara and Richard Brautigan is their use of the poet's own experience as the substance for lyric statement. There is nothing unusual in either of their backgrounds. O'Hara was born (1926) in Baltimore, grew up in Massachusetts, attended Harvard and graduate school at Michigan, and began to publish poetry when he moved to New York and a position at the Museum of Modern Art (he rose to the rank of associate curator, and was about to be named curator when he died July 25, 1966, following an automobile accident). His fame was enhanced by two posthumous volumes, *The Collected Poems of Frank O'Hara* (New York: Alfred A. Knopf, 1971), and *Art Chronicles* (New York: Venture Books/George Braziller, 1975). Brautigan was born (1933) in Tacoma, Washington, where he lived before moving to San Francisco and publishing poetry and fiction with small, experimental presses, later reissued by Dell and other large commercial houses. Although their personal selves are unexceptional, and beyond the fact that each poet relies on a conversational simplicity and almost complete self-effacement of ego as given in his poetry, O'Hara and Brautigan were fortunate to be in the right place at an exceptionally right time: O'Hara in New York City among painters during the ascendant period of Abstract Expressionism, Brautigan in San Francisco during that city's most vital artistic period, just as the Beat movement turned into the Haight-Ashbury "hippie" culture of the 1960s (and before the national media exploited it and diluted its substance as a native community phenomenon). Each drew the larger aesthetic of his poetry from his respective milieu. Because those milieux became the genesis of so much to be adopted later as sixties culture, their poetry is one of the very best indices to the aesthetic spirit of the times.

Frank O'Hara's poetry is exceptionally important for what it tells us about the transformation in American culture, for he based the innovations of his work on three principles: the universal aesthetic being developed among the Abstract Expressionist painters with whom he dealt professionally during evenings at the Cedar Tavern, The Club, and elsewhere; his daily experience in the world of New York culture, which included contact with writers, painters, and musicians; and most emphatically on his own sense of personality, a value the sixties would come to place above all else. All three led to integral notions in O'Hara's poetry and were mutually supportive, especially to the end that poetry would serve "the people." A socially relevant role for the artist had been at the core of Abstract Expressionism since its genesis in the 1930s, when left-leaning American artists found that the programmatic relevance of Soviet realism led to an unreal stereotyping, and that true human expression was less likely to be perverted by ideology if it were freed from the demands of representation. Aware of this historical precedent, O'Hara was able to unscramble a truism: that ideas are inseparable from the people who have them, and that such notions as emergency and crisis can be experienced only "as Personal event, the artist assuming responsibility for being, however accidentally, alive here and now." The role of personal responsibility was made clear to the early Abstract Expressionists by the pressures of social and political catastrophe; in calmer times, Frank O'Hara saw that the same response was the necessary ground for socially meaningful poetry as well.

What was true for painting followed for poetry: once action and gesture were released from the contingencies of representation, they were free to become part of experience, where presumably they would lead a fuller and more useful life. In O'Hara's hands the poem is not a report of experience, nor is it a distillation of experience. The poem is *more experience.* Only as experience can it partake of the personal, and only in the personal is there any chance for artistic value.

"Don't be bored, don't be lazy, don't be trivial, and don't be proud. The slightest loss of attention leads to death," O'Hara says. The greatest danger, as we live our lives in the world, is that the world may become unreal to us. Once that happens, everything else fails. Life becomes banal, insipid, and dull because we cannot relate to it. Because nothing of our ego is projected outward, life is meaningless. Life becomes death. Against this danger of alienation Frank O'Hara offers an aesthetics of attention. Familarity breeds contempt, and so the challenge of his art is to defamiliarize. In O'Hara's poetry the usual objects of daily life are there, but deftly removed from the overly familiar context which tends to kill them. Objects themselves may remain familiar, but if our perception of them becomes routine their animistic value dies. Therefore O'Hara disrupts the usual patterns of our understanding. His poems are formed by discon-

tinuities of texture, forcing the reader to consciously and carefully experience each surface as if for the first time, literally feeling one's way
through the poem. O'Hara recognized this method in the painting of Larry
Rivers which, he said, "taught me to be more keenly interested while I'm
still alive. And perhaps this is the most important thing art can say." It is
certainly the most important service poetry can perform for the reader, a
virtual lifesaving act. In her *Frank O'Hara: Poet Among Painters* (New
York: George Braziller, 1977) Marjorie Perloff has described a typical
O'Hara poem as a "melodic graph of the poet's perception" (p. 123). Its
reception can work the same way. The reader may sing the resulting poem
as a melody precisely because the poet has accomplished the same goal as
the popular songwriter: he has taken familiar objects (notes on a scale,
things one bumps into every day) and arranged them in an unfamiliar but
adoptable order, a strikingly new variation on the given terms of life.
O'Hara's poetry teaches one how to sing existence.

Life is movement, poems like these tell us by their very structure.
O'Hara prefers writing in the present tense, because it is the tense of action.
"It is 12:20 in New York a Friday / three days after Bastille day, yes"
begins one of his most typical poems, "The Day Lady Died." Like an action painter, O'Hara relies on his sense of continuing movement to capture
the reality of experience and tries to make the dance of words in his
sentences as strong and as expressive as the sweep of Franz Kline's arm
across the surface of a canvas, or as vital as the push and pull of graphic
elements in a work by Hans Hofmann. In a syntax formed with such goals
in mind, the word "and" is his favorite connective. It keeps the poem moving forward, keeps it simply *moving,* and where a more rhetorical connective would seem more appropriate, the simple "and" makes a nice non se-
quitur, demanding the reader's attention by its deliberate ruffling of the
poem's surface ("it is 1959 and I go get a shoeshine / because I will get off
the 4:19 in Easthampton / at 7:15 and then go straight to dinner / and I
don't know the people who will feed me").

O'Hara's juxtapositions are lined up all in a row, and where a conventional poet would create a new insight, a third object, by juxtaposing two
otherwise distinct items, the sixties poet plays this game only for a clearer
look at objects one and two. "I walk up the muggy street beginning to sun /
and have a hamburger and a malted and buy / an ugly NEW WORLD
WRITING to see what the poets / in Ghana are doing these days"; no third
reality is created, but the existing elements are seen more distinctly as the
poet draws them out in sequence. His walk down Fifty-third Street has been
expressed in the verbal equivalent to an Abstract Expressionist painter's
sweep of line across a canvas. That line has no reference, and neither do

O'Hara's objects. They defy all conventional notions of structure (they are not there for irony, for paradox, for tension—they are simply *there*). The poet does not want to show us the results of his coming to awareness. The poem is more democratic if it shares with the reader the process of that act, and so judgment is suspended until the poem can run its course, just like the artist's experience. By the 1960s people in American culture were accustomed to having aesthetic perceptions expressed for them in terms of movies or television, and an entire generation had grown up with the experience of continual bombardment by visual images as a more natural form of expression than the old fireside story. Sixties poetry reflects this flow. Process is more important than product, because the real subject is energy. "So much in the making of art is energy," Larry Rivers told O'Hara. "Not just the manipulation of the arm or fingers, but the physical insistence of the mind to keep on making decisions—in spite of the continuous physical and mental disruption." Rivers was originally a jazz musician, in the style of Charlie Parker and Lester Young, whose improvisational lines came the closest to departing from the restrictions of chord structure and the song's melody—until in the 1960s, coincidental with Rivers' strongest art and O'Hara's freest poetry, the new style of jazz played by Ornette Coleman, Don Cherry, and Archie Shepp dispensed with chords and melody altogether in favor of free-form, amorphous jazz.

Among O'Hara's earliest poems are similar free-form experiments, such as "Today":

> Oh! kangaroos, sequins, chocolate sodas!
> You really are beautiful! Pearls,
> harmonicas, jujubes, aspirins! all
> the stuff they've always talked about
>
> still makes a poem a surprise!
> These things are with us every day
> even on beachheads and biers. They
> do have meaning. They're strong as rocks.

In his mature work O'Hara would count off such objects as he went about his business on "The Day Lady Died," for instance, surpassing the playful Dadaism of "Today." But even in the latter poems, the objects kept their own integrity; they stayed as strong as rocks. Abstract Expressionist painters had taught O'Hara that any materials he might use in his creations must exist in their own right. Only because they exist is he considering them for his poem in the first place. But since his poem will not rely on mimetic illusion (an artificially constructed reality), any sense of the real must come from the objects he incorporates. Therefore a respect for materials is foremost, and like the Abstract Expressionists he will put them in intact—as they used bits of cloth and string, even as Jackson Pollock discarded the traditional artist's palette for commercial house paint dripped right onto the surface of his canvas. *A sensuous interest in materials comes first;* this was a judgment O'Hara cited in respect to work by Robert Motherwell. Writing on Jackson Pollock, O'Hara observed, "the artist absorbed or assimilated very few things. They were left intact and given back." Respecting the objectivity is one way of keeping one's self intact; neither pollutes the other. Everything could be itself and still be poetry—such was O'Hara's ideal, and his posture is one of observing and then participating, like a player learning the rules of a game and finally joining in.

"The Day Lady Died" continues with such exploration of rules, such improvisation with the objects likely to be encountered while history transpires:

> I go to the bank
> And Miss Stillwagon (first name Linda I once heard)
> doesn't even look up my balance for once in her life
> and in the GOLDEN GRIFFIN I get a little Verlaine
> for Patsy with drawings by Bonnard although I do
> think of Hesiod, trans. Richmond Lattimore or
> Brendan Behan's new play or *Le Balcon* or *Les Nègres*
> of Genet, but I don't, I stick with Verlaine
> after practically going to sleep with quandariness

The details are purposely petty, as a way of keeping the poem (like an Abstract Expressionist painting) on the surface. It was on the surface, not within the depths of perspective and illusion, where the push and pull of action painting took place, and O'Hara believed he must maintain the same presence of surface in his poetry. "To put it very gently," he wrote with respect to his long poem "Second Avenue," "I have a feeling that the philosophical reduction of reality to a dealable-with system so distorts life that one's 'reward' for this endeavor (a minor one, at that) is illness both from inside and outside." Therefore the verbal elements in his poems

> are intended consciously to keep the surface of the poem high and dry, not wet, reflective and self-conscious. Perhaps the obscurity comes in here, in the relationship between the surface and the meaning, but I like it that way since one is the other (you have to use words) and I hope the poem to *be* the subject, not just about it.

The apparent lack of consequence of O'Hara's verbal objects reflects the same inconsequence of Jackson Pollock's drips, Franz Kline's sweeping lines, Willem de Kooning's swirls of colors—inconsequential by themselves (because they must remain themselves, as objects) but of great importance in tracing the action of the artist's body. Field paintings, as Pollock's are called, deliberately dispense with specific centers of interest so that the eye can follow the painter's hand. Gesture succeeds object, action outweighs image. In poetry, visual imagery gives way to evocations, traceable among the poet's movement from image to image in series, as in a field. The state of the poet's mind is suggested by the action of images within it, moving from Verlaine to Hesiod to Behan to Genet and back to Verlaine again, as he picks out a gift for his dinner hostess on the day Billie Holiday died. The presence of Frank O'Hara in "The Day Lady Died" must be as clear as the presence of Helen Frankenthaler which O'Hara sees in "Towards a New Climate" or any other of her abstract works: "Existing *in* the canvas like stains, it is perfect in detail, revealing extensions of space within and beyond the surface while the actuality of this surface is adamantly contained by the hand of the painter." In poetry, the active presence of O'Hara's psyche pulls the reader into the poem's sense of the present, which *lives* like the intensity of a Pollock or Kline painting.

"Painting is a sheer extension, not a window or a door," we find Frank O'Hara writing in his *Art Chronicles*. It is extension even when it incorporates realistic objects, as happens in the art of collage: "collage is as much about paper as about form" (p. 71). The fact that words are signs referring to real objects or ideas out there in the world is no more an impediment to true abstract expressionism in poetry than are the concrete materials of collage, or even the Duco paint used by Jackson Pollock. From the same page in *Art Chronicles:* "The impetus for a painting or drawing starts technically from the subconscious through automatism (or as he [Robert Motherwell] may say 'doodling') and proceeds toward the subject which is the finished work." In the September 1976 issue of the *Journal of Modern Literature* Fred Moramarco indicates just how "painterly" O'Hara's poetics were. The poem, like the canvas, is "an arena in which to act," to adopt a phrase of Harold Rosenberg from *The Tradition of the New* (New York: Horizon, 1959), "rather than as a space in which to reproduce, redesign, analyze or 'express' an object, actual or imagined. What was to go on the canvas was not a picture but an event" (p. 25). The artist's biography, conscious or unconscious, is of great importance, but it will not be useful in the same way previous aesthetic dispositions found it. Describing "The American Action Painters," Rosenberg made the distinction for the new age:

> a painting that is an act is inseparable from the biography of the artist. The painting itself is a "moment" in the adulterated mixture of his life—whether "moment" means the actual minutes taken up with spotting the canvas or the entire duration of a lucid drama conducted in sign language. (pp. 27–28)

Most important for O'Hara's practice of poetry was Rosenberg's new aesthetic principle that "The act-painting is of the same metaphysical substance as the artist's existence. The new painting has broken down every distinction between art and life" (p. 28). The old rules said that art should deal with universals, while life smothers in its glut of particularities. O'Hara's genius, schooled in the aesthetic of Abstract Expressionism, was to fashion an art made up of the very stuff of life. Its universal grounding was in the life of the human individual.

For O'Hara's art to succeed, words must be placed on the paper not as transcriptions of the writer's thoughts, meant to communicate linguistically with the poem's reader, but rather in what Fred Moramarco calls a painterly way, with "the look and sound of the words and their placement in relation to other words reflecting the meaning and evoked response" (p. 442). The last two stanzas of "The Day Lady Died" reveal this painterly manner:

> and for Mike I just stroll into the PARK LANE
> Liquor Store and ask for a bottle of Strega and
> then I go back where I came from to 6th Avenue
> and the tobacconist in the Ziegfield Theatre and
> casually ask for a carton of Gauloises and a carton
> of Picayunes, and a NEW YORK POST with her face on it
>
> and I am sweating a lot by now and thinking of
> leaning on the john door in the 5 SPOT
> while she whispered a song along the keyboard
> to Mal Waldron and everyone and I stopped breathing

The poem's elements, kept intact by the neutral connective "and," march right on through the poet's day, with no subjective distinction in importance: a bottle of wine for Mike Goldberg, a carton of French cigarettes for Frank O'Hara, a tragic death for Billie Holiday. But the subjective effect, for the reader as well as for the poet, is stunning. By keeping events objective, he has kept them external; and by keeping them external, they can operate with a full sense of life. There is certainly ironic surprise in stumbling into the fact of Lady Day's death so haphazardly between the cigarettes and whatever comes next. But the shock of that contrast has taken the poet—and the reader with him—back to the quintessential moment in Billie Holiday's life, a moment which lived equally for all her listeners. Because O'Hara has incorporated the reader's attention into his bouncy, inconsequential "I do this / I do that" rhythm of existence, he can pull that same attention into the poem's most important part simply by momentum. In this manner Frank O'Hara remains respectful to the objective existence of things in life, while shaping them into works of art.

The scale of Frank O'Hara's poetry is, as he himself described the work of Jackson Pollock, "the physical reality of the artist and his activity of expressing it." Nothing else could be so real. What all the arts in the sixties found was that there was a more perfect reality beyond that found in the polar opposites of documentary representation and deep romantic effusion. O'Hara chose the role which would become a pattern for artists in the sixties, to shape his own life as a work of fiction. He saw this pattern in the work of Larry Rivers, which served as "a diary of his experience," having "chosen to mirror his preoccupations and enthusiasms in an unprogrammatic way." In the end, O'Hara would make no distinction between life and poetry, a personal ethic the sixties could easily adopt as it own. The great cry for the right of personal determination, originating in the ghettoes but most instructive to the culture in the form of middle-class student protest, was in part the need for people to act as the shaping artists of their own lives (much of the student revolution, in fact, was choreographed to rock and roll).

The structure of poetry is in its syntax. Critiquing the work of Franz Kline, O'Hara noted that "The whites and blacks are strokes and masses of entirely relevant intensity to the painting as a whole and to each other. The strokes and linear gestures of the painter's arm and shoulder are aimed at an ultimate structure of feeling rather than at ideograph or writing," and in his own poetry the referential character of objects fades away in proportion to the compositional energy behind them. Syntax transmits that energy, and for O'Hara the desired route is one of speed and surprise. His apparent insouciance creates an instantaneous *now,* an effect much like the technique of painter Philip Guston, who handled light so that it would emanate from the canvas rather than fall on the plane.

The chief components of Frank O'Hara's poetry are the author and the reader—all of his techniques lead to this conclusion. It was the dual principle he admired most in Abstract Expressionist painting, that a good work of art "engages the viewer in its meaning rather than declaring it." Equal parts of perception and participation were the sum of Frank O'Hara's poetry.

The Spring 1964 issue of *Kulchur,* a little magazine whose masthead listed Frank O'Hara (as art editor) and his close friends Joe LeSueur, LeRoi Jones, Gil Sorrentino, and Bill Berkson, included one of the first national publications by a young West Coast writer named Richard Brautigan. "The Post Offices of Eastern Oregon" depended upon several techniques which were to become central in Brautigan's art; indeed, beneath its apparent simple narrative the story consisted of little else but technique, something which would identify Brautigan with O'Hara's poetic method, even though less important aspects would earn him a more popular readership.

Some of Brautigan's "gentle hippie" posings are evident in this early work, which begins as the story of a young boy and his uncle heading off for a day's hunting in the Oregon countryside. This sympathy-earning posture comes from Brautigan's talent for the fresh and appealing image, a thought cast in such unfamiliar shape that no one in the straight culture could be expected to think of it first. The boy and his uncle pass a long-abandoned farmhouse: "Nobody lived there," we are told; "It was abandoned like a musical instrument." Childish fancies mix with brilliant poetic images: "There was a good pile of wood beside the house. Do ghosts burn wood? I guess it's up to them, but the wood was the color of years." Brautigan's story advances on the energy of such images, and achieves its narrative form because so many of the images are extended. "Uncle Jarv had once been a locally famous high school athlete and later on, a legendary honky-tonker. He once had four hotel rooms at the same time and a bottle of whiskey in each room, but they had all left him." When the pair stop at an old house in town, the narrator observes "The house had wooden frosting all around the edges. It was a wedding cake from a previous century. Like candles we were going to stay there for the night." The candles-on-the-cake image is kinesthetic, relying upon the reader's memory to connect it with the wedding-cake trim from the sentences before. In later stories Brautigan would separate such images by paragraphs and even chapters, giving his readers a larger field of play, but even here there is the invitation to participate, an important characteristic of Frank O'Hara's poetry as well.

Other objects pop into the reader's attention and stay there because of Brautigan's attention-getting imagery: mountains teeming with wildcats and cougars, bears served up as cold beers, and the official United States Government wall of an eastern Oregon post office bearing the classic calendar shot of a nude Marilyn Monroe. Hunting seems to be the subject of the story, centered around the boy's anticipations—will there be mountain lions, will there be cougars, will there be wolves, wildcats, or bears? Bears are what the boy and his uncle encounter. Two freshly killed cubs are being unloaded from a pickup truck, and the small talk among Uncle Jarv and his buddies subtly fades into the surreal details of the bear-based economy of this strange little town, where the creatures are roasted, fried, boiled, or made into spaghetti. We are given a few paragraphs of narrative to settle back down into reality (while Uncle Jarv buys a postcard and "filled it up on the counter as if it were a glass of water"), and then the bears disappear, only to be found on the other side of town:

They were on a side street sitting in the front seat of a car. One of the bears had on a pair of pants and a checkered shirt. He was wearing a red hunting hat and had a pipe in the mouth and two paws on the steering wheel like Barney Oldfield.

The other bear had on a white silk negligee, one of the kind you see advertised in the back pages of men's magazines, and a pair of felt slippers stuck on the feet. There was a pink bonnet tied on the head and a purse in the lap.

Somebody opened up the purse, but there wasn't anything inside. I don't know what they expected to find, but they were disappointed. What would a dead bear carry in its purse anyway?

Just at this point, when the story is dpepest into the writer's own private sense of invention and farthest from representational truth, Brautigan shifts modes to bring us his true subject. "Strange is the thing that makes me recall all this again: the bears. It's a photograph in the newspaper of Marilyn Monroe, dead from a sleeping pill suicide, young and beautiful, as they say, with everything to live for." The suddenness of the photo, like the suddenness of death itself, haunts Brautigan, as Frank O'Hara was haunted by his similar chance encounter with the face of Lady Day. "I wonder what post office wall in Eastern Oregon will wear this photograph of Marilyn Monroe?"

Richard Brautigan's writing operates by the same "I do this/I do that" principle as Frank O'Hara's poetry, letting each object or encounter keep the life it had before entering the story, thus releasing the writer from any obligations to invent a counterfeit life within his fiction—life is already there. Brautigan also shares with O'Hara (and in turn with the Abstract Expressionists) a strong sense of textuality. Lines in his book speak back and forth among themselves. His first novel, *A Confederate General from Big Sur* (New York: Grove Press, 1964), offers the information that 425 individuals were appointed to the rank of Confederate general during the Civil War. That data is the substance of Chapter One. Chapter Two is a list of occupations, "Lawyers, jurists / 129, Professional soldiers / 125, Businessmen / 55," and so forth, in response to the chapter-head question, "I Mean, What Do You Do Besides Being a Confederate General?" Brautigan's next two novels, *Trout Fishing in America* (San Francisco: Four Seasons Foundation, 1967) and *In Watermelon Sugar* (San Francisco: Four Seasons Foundation, 1968), use the logotype of their titles as substitutions for more conventional words right within the syntax of the book's sentences. "In Watermelon Sugar, the deeds were done and done again as my life is done in watermelon sugar," the latter novel begins. "Trout Fishing in America" alternates as a book, as a character, and as an idea, being the major unifying element in a collection of otherwise disorganized short chapters. The author tells us he always hoped to end a novel with the word "mayonnaise," and so the last page, an inconsequential letter of bereavement bearing little relevance to anything else in the book, ends "P. S./Sorry I forgot to give you the mayonaise," with the key word comically misspelled. A similar randomness pervades the full breadth of Brautigan's writing; as with O'Hara's poetry, we are expected to follow his chain of unexpected associations for their very freshness of unfamiliarity. The poet's art of surprise can make a boring world live for us again.

Brautigan builds his images by such apparent randomness, and he selects materials with the brilliant serendipity of the artists who so impressed Frank O'Hara. In *Trout Fishing in America* the narrator's stepfather speaks of trout as if they are a precious metal, but because the man is an old drunk, the boy's impression is more like steel than gold or silver. "Maybe trout steel. Steel made from trout. The clear snow-filled river acting as a foundry and heat. Think of Pittsburgh. A steel that comes from trout, used to make buildings, trains and tunnels. The Andrew Carnegie of Trout!" (p. 3). Only a respect for the individuality of materials can produce such images, as for the Big Sur, a "thousand-year-old flophouse for mountain lions and lilacs," or a birthmark "which looked just like an old car parked on his head." Like the bears in the post office story, such fiercely independent components keep Brautigan's images from running off as references to the real world; their independent objectiveness keeps them riveted to the page as proof of the artist's act in joining them.

The synthesizing powers of the imagination are often the subject of Brautigan's fiction, such as in the John Dillinger Museum which forms a chapter of *Trout Fishing in America,* or the character in the same book named Trout Fishing in America Shorty, a paraplegic wino so tritely dull that Brautigan proposes shipping him back to the writer who made all such characters cliches, Nelson Algren. The imaginative transformation of reality is shown to be just as possible for individuals as it is for general aspects of the culture, which through commercial use and abuse get changed into absurd excuses for the actual world.

Yet *Trout Fishing in America* is less about philosophical matters than it is, quite simply, about itself. Brautigan's far-reaching metaphors are wacky comparisons which stretch the maximum distance between tenor and vehicle so that the reader must made a hardy effort to connect the two. In this way the book comes together in the reader's mind as a living structure. It is a book about words, and Brautigan has fun with them. A warning sign, for example reads

NO TRESPASSING
4/17 OF A HAIKU

But the real action is performed by the reader making sense of Brautigan's language, for it is the kinesthetic effect of pondered language which makes the novel live. "The other graveyard was for the poor and it had no trees and the grass turned a flat-tire brown in the summer and stayed that way until the rain, like a mechanic, began in the late autumn"; "Eventually the seasons would take care of their wooden names [on the grave markers] like a sleepy short-order cook cracking eggs over a grill next to a railroad station"; "Knowing that the trout would wait there like airplane tickets for us to come"—the lyricism of these comparisons is a poetry in motion, and the motion is that of the reader's mind moving from point to point in the complex image Brautigan's language provides.

In addition to working the imaginative mechanics which make these metaphors live, the reader is obliged to extend them—adopting them, as it were, into his or her own vocabulary. A trout stream is measured in terms of Victorian telephone booths, then a page later the narrator wades in to a distance of "about seventy-three telephone booths"; "The chub made an awkward dead splash and obeyed all the traffic laws of this world SCHOOL ZONE SPEED 25 MILES and sank to the cold bottom of the lake. It lay there white belly up like a school bus covered with snow. A trout swam over and took a look, just putting in time, and swam away" (p. 71). Other images are alternately visceral and lyrical, suggesting a body English with which the reader may move through them, such as "a ukelele . . . pulled like a plow through the intestines," or "we drove out of the sheep like an airplane flies out of the clouds."

Imagination, properly employed, can animate a vignette such as the John Dillinger Museum in Mooresville, Indiana, or simply liven up a person's life, according to the rules prescribed in the chapter, "Sea, Sea Rider." But most impressive in Brautigan's writing is his ability to compose absurdly fantastic narratives out of mundane materials as easy to accept as reality itself. *In Watermelon Sugar* speaks in familiar terms about unfamiliar events, assembling them in a collage which gives full recognition to each component while constructing a new reality bearing no relation at all to its parts:

> 3: The tigers and how they lived and how beautiful they were and how they died and how they talked to me while they ate my parents, and how I talked back to them and how they stopped eating my parents, though it did not help my parents any, nothing could help them by then, and we talked for a long time and one of the tigers helped me with my arithmetic, then they told me to go away while they finished eating my parents, and I went away. I returned later that night to burn the shack down. That's what we did in those days. (p. 8)

Like any poet, Richard Brautigan's words create a lyrical space between the reader and the world. His special achievement, apparent
elsewhere in the general movement of sixties culture, was to phrase that
lyricism in words allowed to exist independently of the things they symbol-
ized in the actual world. O'Hara and Brautigan were able to become artists
in their own right, a notable achievement in art forms previously chained to
the limits of secondhand expression. The world could indeed be reinvented,
once we were no longer chained to the falsely absolute meaning of words
themselves.

CHAPTER FOUR

Kurt Vonnegut and Donald Barthelme: The American Image

It is in the nature of their work that American novelists frame an image of America. Their fictions take place in a world which must be recognizable, but a world also defined and shaped by art. The locale of Nathaniel Hawthorne's fiction, for example, shares a topical identity with the country colonized by Pilgrims and Puritans; but once expressed in art it takes on imaginative qualities which historians can find otherwise only by a deep-searching study of the times. How a novelist shapes reality is important in finding out how a culture views itself, for the structure of a writer's vision in these cases may reflect the imagination of his or her times.

For Hawthorne, American life was a tension between light and dark, daytime and night, the village and the forest, ambition and anxiety, innocence and guilt, good and evil—his fictional view of the world was structured by these polarities, just as Herman Melville's characterization of the age was cast in terms of Captain Ahab's Faustian challenge against the universe itself. In similar manner, Mark Twain's work spoke of a very civilized era's promptings toward the freedom and vulgarity of the wilderness, while William Dean Howells found within that same rapidly stratifying society an understandable structure for the image Americans had of themselves. In our own century, F. Scott Fitzgerald has come to symbolize the twenties, just as the mention of John Steinbeck calls forth a picture of the social and economic turmoils in the thirties. Each writer so completely and convincingly described an image for the times that any of his books, or even he himself, could be cited as a fair respresentation of the period in question.

Kurt Vonnegut has emerged as the signal writer for the sixties, largely because he had formed his own apprentice fiction in the sentiments from previous decades and by the 1960s was able to develop simultaneously and sympathetically with the new age. Vonnegut has claimed repeatedly that the greatest influences on his fiction were his common American experiences, reaching from his childhood among a big, happy family in the Middle West, through the trauma of the Great Depression (a deeper catastrophe for most Americans than even World War II), college, combat experience in the war, and peacetime service in the ranks of white-collar Americans working for the big corporations in the late 1940s. His artistic models were unashamedly popular writers (Robert Louis Stevenson, Edgar Lee Masters) and the great radio and film comedians of the thirties: Jack Benny, Fred Allen, Laurel and Hardy. Benny and his contemporaries were able to create an image for America during those hard times which allowed the country, without any contradictions, to sustain itself and eventually prosper. Vonnegut insists that artists share the same responsibility now, and it was with this explicitly social role in mind that he began his career as a writer.

His first efforts were for a closely defined market, the weekly family magazines of the 1950s, and Vonnegut was careful to frame his own vision in terms average Americans could understand. Between 1950 and 1963 Kurt Vonnegut published over fifty stories in such large-circulation magazines as *Collier's, The Saturday Evening Post, Redbook, Cosmopolitan,* and even *Ladies Home Journal* and *Better Homes and Gardens.* His success indicates he had found a winning formula, a structure appealing to and reflective of America's popular image of itself during these years (part of Vonnegut's postwar graduate study in anthropology had been on the ability of short stories to describe the shape of their originating culture).

Looking back at these short fictions two decades later, we can see how Vonnegut gauged the culture and, more significantly, the direction in which it was heading. At their simplest, his stories reaffirm certain satisfying notions middle-class Americans might have about themselves: that simple virtue outweighs and outlasts more sophisticated pretentions, that there can be such a thing as too high a price for success, that the poor can often be happier than the rich. Of course, Vonnegut expresses it all with a twist. "A Present for Big Nick" (*Argosy,* December 1954) tells how a group of children lead a bloody rebellion against a hated and feared figure, Santa Claus (who in fact is their fathers' gangster-employer dressed up for a bullyish and vexing Christmas party). In "Hal Irwin's Magic Lamp" (*Cosmopolitan,* June 1957) a husband strikes it rich and gives his wife a genie who answers every wish, including a return to poverty (via the Great Depression) when the money spoils their happiness. The middle-class self-image of the fifties, Vonnegut learned, was so established as an institution that it could entertain its own satire, even in such complacent magazines as *Collier's* and the *Post.* Moreover, the times were ready for more serious criticism of suburban development ("Poor Little Rich Town," *Collier's,* October 25, 1952), self-serving technology ("Unready to Wear," *Galaxy,* April 1953), and the absurdity of war ("The Manned Missiles," *Cosmopolitan,* July 1958). Automation's threat to human values is another important critique, both in Vonnegut's stories and his first novel, *Player*

Piano (1952). By the decade's end, he was stretching his vision to cosmic proportions in *The Sirens of Titan* (1959), which reordered earthly notions from a higher perspective, both interplanetary and theological. Kurt Vonnegut was ready for the sixties.

"Call me Jonah," begins *Cat's Cradle* (New York: Holt, Rinehart & Winston, 1963), Vonnegut's first novel to define American culture in terms of the developing decade. "Jonah—John—if I had been a Sam, I would have been a Jonah still—not because I have been unlucky for others, but because somebody or something has compelled me to be certain places at certain times, without fail," the narrator named John tells us. He has tried to write a book titled *The Day the World Ended,* about the atomic bombing of Hiroshima in World War II, but his search for material leads him to a much larger subject, the day the world actually does end. A joint military/scientific venture causes that catastrophe as well—in Vonnegut's book the weaponry even has the same inventor—but the novel's range of vision goes beyond the march-to-destruction theme which groups such as SANE (National Committee for a Sane Nuclear Policy) were protesting in the streets. *Cat's Cradle* takes on such notions as patriotism, national identity, the nature of love, free will, and the meaning of life as it proceeds to find a new shape for the culture's imagination. The old shape, we are told, has taken the form of a death wish, and the only hope for survival is a reordering of the universe of values which Vonnegut takes up for reconsideration.

Adapting itself to the new sixties aesthetic, *Cat's Cradle* uses a realistic sense of textuality so that the reader can accept the book as a valid artifact and not a fairy story calling for the suspension of disbelief (and, in the process, the suspension of all pertinence as well). As we meet him, the narrator is writing a book. His problem getting his job done becomes the book in our hands, which we can accept as a valid object in the world because we have seen it made and even have participated in its making. There are no lies, no illusions; the reading and writing of *Cat's Cradle* are frank, open business. Such complicity is needed for the novel-as-reality to work, since Vonnegut is proposing nothing less than a fundamental reordering of our view of existence. For example, the political distinctions which so control human society are shown to be meaningless. "Pay no attention to Caesar," says Bokonon, the novel's religious prophet, "Caesar doesn't have the slightest idea what's *really* going on" (p. 88). Like his younger colleagues, Richard Brautigan and Donald Barthelme, and especially like his contemporary, Joseph Heller, Vonnegut has the talent to expose the bogus nature of what commonly passes for reality in contemporary American culture so effectively that he can get readers to distrust their deepest feeling of what makes sense and what is absurd.

The first major restructuring of vision in *Cat's Cradle* concerns the military use of science. Through World War II, President Truman's announcement and justification of the Hiroshima bombing, and the build-up of a nuclear arsenal in the 1950s, Americans as a rule did not question the legitimacy of atomic weapons. When there were debates on the subject, positions were simply pro or con, with each side easily stereotyped. Vonnegut now drew the problem in completely new dimensions. The scientist in *Cat's Cradle* who supposedly invents the bomb, Dr. Felix Hoenikker, is neither a bloodthirsty monster nor a savior to mankind. At first he appears as nothing but a foolish old dolt, scarcely distinguishable in brainpower from his young children. "I can remember cold mornings," his son Newt recalls, "when Father, Frank and I would be all in a line in the front hall, and Angela would be bundling us up, treating us exactly the same. Only I was going to kindergarten; Frank was going to junior high; and Father was going to work on the atom bomb" (p. 23). As a scientist, Hoenikker is fascinated by toys and gimmicks, and at one point is so taken with the neck-retractability of dime-store turtles that his work on the bomb sits completely forgotten. "Some people from the Manhattan Project finally came out to the house to ask Angela what to do," Newt reports. "She told them to take away Father's turtles. So one night they went into his laboratory and stole the turtles and the aquarium. Father never said a word about the disappearance of the turtles. He just came to work the next day and looked for things to play with and think about, and everything there was to play with and think about had something to do with the bomb" (p. 24).

Just when the silly old man is about to become a comic character, Vonnegut undercuts him with something darkly tragic. Driving to work one day he gets stuck in traffic and abandons his car to walk, another instance of his winsome absent-mindedness. But his wife must retrieve the abandoned vehicle. She is not used to driving it and has a serious accident, suffering an injury which later kills her in childbirth. As readers, we are caught laughing in the face of horror; the man was not so winsome after all. And all this time, moreover, we have been seduced into laughing along with the conscienceless man who created the atomic bomb. Conclusions of guilt or innocence, right or wrong, are not so easily drawn, Vonnegut shows us. He has also discredited our own ways of making such decisions. Coming to terms with the reality of nuclear destruction calls for a new way to view the world, and for a new image of ourselves. Vonnegut was not alone in suggesting this change. In the film *Dr. Strangelove, or How I Learned to Stop Worrying and Love the Bomb,* Terry Southern, Peter George, and Stanley Kubrick undertook a similar reordering, contrary to the lingering fifties' style of thinking in such stereotyped books and films as *Fail-Safe* and *Seven Days in May.*

Other conventional notions are challenged in like manner. Against the notion of war's noble sacrifice, and the way we celebrate it, one character in *Cat's Cradle* proposes that "Perhaps, when we remember wars, we should take off our clothes and paint ourselves blue and go around on all fours all day long and grunt like pigs. That would surely be more appropriate than noble oratory and shows of flags and well-oiled guns" (p. 206). In the 1960s Vonnegut was a sought-after campus speaker, often for commencements where the students could choose their own. In these circumstances, Vonnegut told them similar iconoclastic, image-rebuilding things: what a great swindle it was that they were expected to go change the world, and—on a topic close to the nature of *Cat's Cradle*—how stupid it was to claim God's endorsement of any mortal project. With the same authority as Bob Dylan singing of the opposing armies marching off to war "with God on their side," Vonnegut argued that "Earthlings who have felt that the Creator clearly wanted this or that have almost always been pigheaded and cruel. You bet."

Vonnegut's real intent, however, is to reorder our perception of the world, to revalue our basis for meaning, and for such purposes a novel is more effective than a public speech. As the embodiment of imagination itself, a work like *Cat's Cradle* is a new reality in practice. Anything and everything which happens in the novel is an object lesson in rearranging one's values and perceptions. When a ship breaks up off the reef surrounding San Lorenzo, the island where the novel's action concludes, its cargo of wicker furniture and colony of rats are washed ashore. "So some people got free furniture, and some people got bubonic plague." That is how things happen to happen, and a search for any deeper meaning is fruitless. Of course, there is the opportunity for humane action. The existentialist world view of previous decades would urge the islanders to roll up their shirt sleeves, organize medical teams, and fight the plague to the death. But the measure and scope of death have changed in this postatomic world. One character, Dr. Julian Castle, does build a hospital in the jungle and labor night and day to save the plague's victims, but so many have died "that a bulldozer actually stalled trying to shove them toward a common grave," the doctor's son reports. When even existentialism is discredited as a workable philosophy, Dr. Castle finds a new one. He begins to giggle. "He couldn't stop," his son tells the narrator. "He walked out into the night with his flashlight. He was still giggling. He was making the flashlight beam dance over all the dead people stacked outside. He put his hand on my head and do you know what that marvelous man said to me?" Philip Castle answers his own question. " 'Son,' my father said to me, 'someday this will all be yours' " (p. 135).

The conditions on San Lorenzo, which vaguely echo developing conditions of the sixties in general, demand the reinvention of reality. Religion is one such reinvention, and for San Lorenzo Vonnegut concocts a dandy. "Bokononism," like sixties art itself, is built on selfconscious play and the rejection of all aesthetic illusion. *No damn cat, no damn cradle"* is the refrain which leads to the novel's title, but it is also the central truth of Vonnegut's mock religion. Religion is indeed an opiate, and a very necessary one, especially under modern conditions where the opiate of the people is more likely to become opium. In San Lorenzo, "religion became the one real instrument of hope. Truth was the enemy of the people, because the truth was so terrible, so Bokonon made it his business to provide the people with better and better lies" (p. 143). The novelty in Vonnegut's new dispensation is that the people know the religion consists of lies. And even though it doesn't improve the material standard of living one bit, the people are happy. The truth can be comfortably ignored, because "they were all employed full time as actors in a play they understood, that any human being anywhere could understand and applaud." The narrator marvels at this new approach to reality: "So life became a work of art!" (p. 144).

The Bokononist religion allows its adherents to live happy, satisfying lives of fiction—aesthetic constructs in which they share a part of the making. The application to sixties culture, Vonnegut points out, is in terms even broader than religion. Properly written, novels can provide the same revitalizing function; several times in *Cat's Cradle* the writer's job is described as making analgesics for the world's pain, and the alternatives to "the consolations of literature" are listed as "petrescence of the heart or atrophy of the nervous system" (the chapter is entitled "A Medical Opinion on the Effects of a Writers' Strike"). Much is made of the *foma,* or "harmless untruths," of the Bokononist religion, and the dustjacket of Vonnegut's novel bears evidence that the author considers his writing to be a similar act. On that jacket's design the term "a novel" is footnoted as "a harmless untruth."

Two parables (or "calypsoes") of Bokonon tell why fiction-making is one of the most important human activities. One reads:

> Tiger got to hunt,
> Bird got to fly;
> Man got to sit and wonder, "Why, why, why?"
> Tiger got to sleep,
> Bird got to land;
> Man got to tell himself he understand. (p. 150)

The second is fundamental to Vonnegut's reconstitution of man's role in the universe and lies at the heart of the sixties' new aesthetic purpose for fiction:

In the beginning, God created the earth, and he looked upon it in His cosmic loneliness.

And God said, "Let Us making living creatures out of mud, so the mud can see what We have done." And God created every living creature that now moveth, and one was man. Mud as man alone could speak. God leaned close as mud as man sat up, looked around, and spoke. Man blinked. "What is the *purpose* of all this?" he asked politely.

"Everything must have a purpose?" asked God.

"Certainly," said man.

"Then I leave it to you to think of one for all of this," said God. And He went away. (pp. 214–215)

Kurt Vonnegut's fiction of the 1960s exists as demonstrations of the Bokononist fiction-making principle. *Cat's Cradle* admittedly is set in a microcosmic world of a Caribbean island, where the large issues of life and meaning can be manageably engaged. In his next novel, *God Bless You, Mr. Rosewater* (New York: Holt, Rinehart & Winston, 1965), Vonnegut shows how his same aesthetic beliefs can be usefully applied to the social reality of the United States. Again his conditions are artificial—his protagonist, Eliot Rosewater, is a multimillionaire, able to effect just about anything on a material scale—but only to point out the moral lesson; a solid role for aesthetics is the key to Vonnegut's design. Eliot takes over his family's charitable foundation in order to revise its function, to redefine and vitalize it in terms of lives actually being lived. He closes down the Rosewater Foundation's Park Avenue offices and moves them to a shotgun attic above a liquor store and lunch counter in Rosewater, Indiana, a pallid postage stamp of land deep within the family's Midwestern holdings. There he tries to effectively help the poor, the abandoned, and the distressed—the supposedly worthless people whom modern conditions have made obsolete. "I'm going to love these discarded Americans," Eliot announces, "even though they're useless and unattractive. *That* is going to be my work of art" (p. 47).

The people of Rosewater County receive Eliot's kindness, but the person helped most is Eliot himself, for he is the one rebuilding his life as a perfect fiction. Not simply the ineffectiveness of the Rosewater Foundation, but also the evil he has seen in war and the malevolence he knows lies at the source of the Rosewater millions convince him that his life needs to be reinvented. The reading of science-fiction novels first gives him hope that this is possible, and that the act can have real meaning. He runs off to a convention of SF writers at Milford, Pennsylvania (an actual conference founded by Damon Knight), where he praises the writers as "the only ones with guts enough to *really* care about the future, who *really* notice what machines do to us, what wars do to us, what cities do to us, what big, simple ideas do to us." He quotes a novel by Kilgore Trout, Vonnegut's SF writer-manqué, who at the end of an apocalyptical novel about the eclipse of human values asks, "What in hell are people *for?*" Vonnegut asks the same question in his own story, "Welcome to the Monkey House." But then Eliot demonstrates just how provisional reality is, how its arbitrary conventions can be restructured at the merest need. He writes a batch of $300 checks, distributes them to the writers, and points his lesson. "*There's* fantasy for you," Eliot says, "And you go to the bank tomorrow, and it will all come true. It's insane that I should be able to do such a thing, with money so important." His imperative to the science-fiction writers is, "think about the silly ways money gets passed around now, and then think up better ways" (p. 31).

In the last chapter of *God Bless You, Mr. Rosewater* Kilgore Trout steps forth as the embodiment of a novelist who can reinvent his own sense of values and improve the general human condition at the same time. His method is the same as Vonnegut's: reexamining the facts of life to see how they have changed, then modifying our perception of that reality in order to make life more meaningful. "Americans have long been taught to hate all people who will not or cannot work, to hate even themselves for that," Trout explains. "We can thank the vanished frontier for that piece of commonsense cruelty. The time is coming, if it isn't here now, when it will no longer be common sense. It will simply be cruel" (p. 210). How do you love people who have no use, who cannot be valued as producers of goods or performers of services once machines have taken over all those tasks? A new perception of human values is in order and Trout's fiction making provides the structure. Significantly, when Vonnegut conspires to have Kilgore Trout win the Nobel Prize (in *Breakfast of Champions,* published in 1973), it is not in literature, but in medicine—for demonstrating the pathological function of ideas in human health and conduct.

Art, in conventional terms, had failed Eliot Rosewater. The fact is mentioned several times. And so he became his own artist, his own novelist, rewriting his own life as a piece of fiction in which the role he plays is noble, helpful, and brave. In so doing he devised a new system of aesthetics. That system is given its fullest test in Vonnegut's next novel, *Slaughterhouse-Five* (New York: Delacorte Press/Seymour Lawrence, 1969), where both Eliot and Trout appear as characters, contributing to the aesthetic Billy Pilgrim will use to make life meaningful again. Vonnegut himself viewed *Slaughterhouse-Five* as a culmination in his own life of fiction. It was a coming to terms with a great traumatic event in his life, the World War II firebombing of Dresden which he experienced as a prisoner of the Germans, but which he was unable to express in fiction through twenty-five years of trying. One problem was in visualizing the firebombing itself. The conventions of his forties and fifties culture did not provide much latitude for portraying large military actions; they inevitably turned out as grand, heroic enterprises. Moreover, war stories became things neatly tucked away in the past, to be recalled with drinking buddies over beer and brandy, but offering no real threat to the comfortable life one now enjoyed. Before the 1960s, there seemed no sure way to capture the disorganizing effect war could have on one's notion of reality—until Joseph Heller found the syntax for it in *Catch-22*, and Kurt Vonnegut followed with a complementary restructuring of time and space in *Slaughterhouse-Five*.

Vonnegut's war novel is his most complete reinvention of the world. It encompasses his experience of four decades, for the book considers not just Billy Pilgrim's adventure in World War II, but his childhood before it and his adult life after it. Billy lives all these moments simultaneously, building his self-image much as any conventional American in the sixties might, having been raised on a diet of Saturday-afternoon movies and sustained with even greater doses of TV. Still, *Slaughterhouse-Five* was the first popular American novel to completely abandon the traditional notions of linear time and solidly fixable space, though people had been living in such imaginative modes for at least a decade. Once Billy learns this new secret of life, he is anxious to tell his countrymen the good news, for by living out of synchronization with the times their lives have become frustrating and disappointing. An optometrist by profession, "He was doing nothing less now, he thought, than prescribing corrective lenses for Earthling souls. So many of those souls were lost and wretched, Billy believed because they could not see as well as his little green friends on Tralfamadore" (p. 25).

The Tralfamadorian viewpoint, easily mistaken as a satirical piece of space opera, is nothing less than Vonnegut's reinvention of the contemporary American novel. Its notion that all time is continually present, that there is no linear progression to reality but that it all exists at once, to be absorbed completely and travelled in at will, is reflected in the form of the Tralfamadorian novel, a description which fits Vonnegut's work (and Barthelme's and Brautigan's and Heller's) as well:

> each clump of symbols is a brief, urgent message—describing a situation, a scene. We Tralfamadorians read them all at once, not one after the other. There isn't any particular relationship between all the messages, except that the author has chosen them carefully, so that, when seen all at once, they produce an image of life that is beautiful and surprising and deep. There is no beginnning, no middle, no end, no suspense, no moral, no causes, no effects. What we love in our books are the depths of many marvelous moments seen all at one time. (p. 76)

A great deal of *Slaughterhouse-Five* is given over to speculations on novels and their therapeutic, recreative power. Billy Pilgrim and Eliot Rose-

water have found life meaningless because of the horrors they have wit-
nessed during the war, "So they were trying to re-invent themselves and
their universe. Science fiction was a big help." At one point in the evolution
of human culture Dostoevsky's *The Brothers Karamazov* told everything
one needed to know about life. " 'But that isn't enough any more,' said
Rosewater" (p. 87). A new perspective is needed for the new cultural conditions of the sixties, Vonnegut knows, and so he spends a fair amount of
time showing all the options. The sum total of those options would be his
own life's work, but to get it all into one book Vonnegut calls on his mythical alter ego, Kilgore Trout, whose hundred-odd novels can be described in
a few lines each. Like his contemporary, Jorge Luis Borges, Vonnegut ap-
preciates how merely talking about a book as if it existed can be as good as
writing the whole work himself. One is Kilgore Trout's *Maniacs in the
Fourth Dimension,* about the need for broader perspectives in medicine. It
turns out that many people suffering from incurable diseases are actually
sick in the fourth dimension; "Earthling doctors couldn't see those causes
at all, or even imagine them." Another is Trout's *The Gospel from Outer
Space,* which argues that the Christian liturgy is confused, and that having
God reveal Christ as His Son only teaches the people that *"Before you kill
somebody, make absolutely sure he isn't well connected."* Trout reinvents
the religion by making Christ a nobody, and the people are in this manner
warned that God *"will punish horribly anybody who torments a bum who
has no connections!"* People need new definitions, "wonderful *new* lies,"
as Eliot Rosewater calls them, "or people just aren't going to want to go on
living." Novels are the handiest repository for such lies—especially novels
which admit their own artificiality.

Vonnegut must also invent a new form for fiction, because the subject
matter of Dresden—of death itself—simply cannot be handled within the
old conventions. "Sam—Here's the book," Vonnegut tells his publisher in
the first chapter. "It is so short and jumbled and jangled, Sam, because
there is nothing intelligent to say about a massacre." Trying to say something, Vonnegut learned, too often results in false heroics or sentimentality.
But then again there are times when one must speak, even when there is no
answer. The moment is dramatized for us at the bedside of Billy's dying
mother, who after several suspenseful moments of stuttering manages to
voice the unanswerable question, "How did I get so old?" What in hell are
people *for?* Vonnegut's fiction revolves in silence at these unanswered
points.

The redefinitions Vonnegut offers are substantial: that the notion of
free will has been a cruel swindle, that existence is in fact fully determined
and utterly meaningless, that life and death coexist in one eternal moment.

But it is not his purpose to be nihilistic. Quite the contrary, by relieving man of responsibility for the mechanical function of existence, Vonnegut frees him to construct whatever arbitrary meaning he desires, in full knowledge that whatever he invents is equally harmless and satisfying. Only because art itself is free of such responsibilities can it do its job. How we perceive reality is what matters, because imagination comes first. To show how, Vonnegut takes a World War II action movie and runs it backwards through the projector. All the destruction is reversed: bombs fall upwards, shrinking and containing the explosions and fires within them. The planes fly backwards to England, where the cannisters are removed and shipped back to the United States, so factory workers can dismantle them, separating the contents into minerals. "The minerals were then shipped to specialists in remote areas. It was their business to put them into the ground, to hide them cleverly, so they would never hurt anybody ever again" (p. 64).

There is a world possible beyond the tyrannies of linear time, cause and effect, and the awful responsibility of free will. Those factors only assume importance when the imagination makes them the almighty rulers of life. The human mind, Vonnegut tells us, is far richer than the body, and by giving it a role in keeping with its power, life can become a much more liveable affair. The aesthetic discipline is not easy, but the ironies lie in how passively and for how long such tyrannical conditions were tolerated. To relent here is not pessimistic, but rather optimistic toward the true human future. As Vonnegut revealed in his preface to the reissued works of Louis-Ferdinand Céline (New York: Penguin Books, 1975):

> I only now understand what I took from Céline and put into the novel I was writing at the time, which was called *Slaughterhouse-Five*. In that book, I felt the need to say this everytime a character died: "So it goes." This exasperated many critics, and it seemed fancy and tiresome to me, too. But somehow it had to be said.
>
> It was a clumsy way of saying what Céline managed to imply so much more naturally in everything he wrote, in effect: "Death and suffering can't matter nearly as much as I think they do. Since they are so common, my taking them so seriously must mean that I am insane. I must try to be saner." (p. xvii)

Death is awful. But it is so common. Through his reinvention of reality, updating it to present standards of existence, Vonngeut's fiction holds us together in a world which might otherwise tear us apart.

The Tralfamadorian novel, with its fragmentary paragraphs defying all traditional conventions and existing outside the continuum of linear time, is nothing other than Vonnegut's description of the appropriate form for fiction in the American 1960s. He discovered a small-press writer successful with this form, Richard Brautigan, and brought his novels to the attention of his own publishers, Seymour Lawrence and the Delacorte Press, who mass-marketed Brautigan's books in handsome trade editions and as ubiquitous Dell paperbacks. And Vonnegut became an appreciative reader (and subsequently close friend) of another younger writer, Donald Barthelme, who was developing as America's leading avant-garde fictionist in the unlikely pages of *The New Yorker* magazine.

For three decades *The New Yorker* had published what might be called typical stories of the times; for each period, *The New Yorker* story could be expected to portray the typical interests, expressed in the momentarily popular manner of the nationwide upper-middle-class audience which formed the magazine's readership. In the 1930s and 1940s this role had been filled by John O'Hara. Whether of small town Pennsylvania or big city New York, his short fictions of the time were sustained by a cultural ambience which made them as natural and familiar as the tunes played on popular radio, or the faces one would meet each day. Lesser writers tried to mimic the form, but O'Hara was its master. In the fifties John Updike joined *The New Yorker* staff, writing for the "Talk of the Town" column up front and, with increasing regularity, contributing short stories to the center of the magazine. His fiction spoke to the evolving times: of young marrieds renting apartments or redecorating suburban homes, of recent graduates struggling for corporate success, of wives who drove station wagons to the shopping center and worried about birth control. Much of Updike's work surpassed this formulaic mode, and he was content to share the "*New Yorker* story" image with another superior writer, John Cheever. Together they set the style for the more seriously written popular short fiction of the late fifties and sixties. Up to 1963, Updike and Cheever were the best artistic models for what the sociology of the period was about.

In 1963 Donald Barthelme began publishing in *The New Yorker*—first with some bright and witty parodies, scarcely distinguishable from the "Talk of the Town" banter and humorous column fillers the magazine was known for. But by 1964 he had hit his stride of six major stories per year—a better pace than Updike's—which he maintained well into the 1970s when attention to novel writing and teaching reduced his output somewhat. Like Updike, Barthelme contributed unsigned pieces to the magazine's front section as well. His regular appearances in *The New Yorker* let him educate a readership to the intricacies of innovative fiction. By the end of the sixties Barthelme was being described as the most imitated short fictionist in America, and his stories (and way of writing them) gave a good indication of the decade's aesthetic inclination, part of which he had shaped himself.

Most apparently, Barthelme is able to deal successfully with the fragments of our present-day lives. His most representative stories, such as "Robert Kennedy Saved from Drowning" (collected in *Unspeakable Practices, Unnatural Acts,* 1968) and "Views of My Father Weeping" (from *City Life,* 1970), are composed of Tralfamadorian-like "clumps"—independent paragraphs whose principle of relation is more spatial than linear, because their effect depends upon the longer and wider view of the reader who considers them all at once, rather than in a sequential order building to a point. This new method was appropriate for the sixties, where a sometimes maddening pluralism of stimuli competed to give us our information. In turn, sixties culture came to distrust the conventional single viewpoint; how could just one angle account for the complexities we knew were present, and how could one viewpoint boast the authority to represent all that might possibly exist? Even more compelling was the suspicion that contradictory arguments might each in their own way be true. For instance, was Robert Kennedy a hero or a villain? And who could hope to sum up or even pin down so enigmatic a person? Barthelme's story reflects these concerns in its structure and offers a way of knowing Robert Kennedy consistent with the feelings of the age. In "Robert Kennedy Saved from Drowning" no one speaks as sole authority. Instead we are given the complex and sometimes contradictory reports of secretaries, aides, associates, and enemies—even a bartender who has to shoo away the Senator from behind the bar during a party. Barthelme feels no compulsion to organize these fragments into a coherent whole. Indeed, such manipulation implies the making of untruths, and certainly runs the risk of losing the authority of Kennedy's presence within these random notes. So they are left as is, even the rough outtakes and the bad snapshots. Like the best of sixties art, there is no illusion of masterwork. The props and scaffolding are left for us to see, partly to satisfy our hope that the truth might be found among them.

For Barthelme, there is always the sense that the ultimate reality lies in structure. And since the ultimate structural element of fiction is found in words, Barthelme's attention becomes almost lexical. One of his first *New Yorker* contributions was "Down the Line with the Annual," a collage of *Consumer Report* language which comically implies a rather tenuous existence for mankind:

> The world is sagging, snagging, scaling, spalling, pilling, pinging, pitting, warping, checking, fading, chipping, cracking, yellowing, leaking, staling, shrinking, and in dynamic unbalance, and there is mildew to think about, and ruptures, and fractures of internal organs from lap belts, and substandard brake fluids, and plastic pipes alluring to rats, and transistor radios whose estimated battery life, like the life of man, is nasty, brutish, and short. (March 21, 1964, p. 34)

Sometimes his structures are larger, as for the scenario notes in a new-wave film called "L'Lapse" ("Shabby pigeons whirl about meaningfully") and in the unusual form of "Man's Face," forty coaxial chapters (all on a single page) of a novel written in the form of *TV Guide* program notes. The best of these early parodies are assembled in the volume *Guilty Pleasures* (1974). But even in his strongest stories, such as those reprinted in *Unspeakable Practices, Unnatural Acts* (New York: Farrar, Straus and Giroux, 1968), Barthelme relies on structure for his greatest effect. "Report" tells about a convention of military scientists, whose weapons sound all too familiar: "We have hypodermic darts capable of piebalding the enemy's pigmentation. We have rots, blights, and rusts capable of attacking his alphabet. Those are dandies." There are even software experts in computer technology. "Consider for instance the area of realtime online computer-controlled wish evaporation," they say. "Wish evaporation is going to be crucial in meeting the rising expectations of the world's peoples, which are as you know rising entirely too fast" (pp. 54–55). The subject sounds plausible, even familiar, though a closer look at its constituents shows how ridiculously mad it all is. How much of our life, Barthelme ponders, adds up to such meaningless exchanges? So he wakes us up to these absurdities of form by dropping in an obviously absurd content, waking us up and shaking in some truth.

Stories like "The Indian Uprising" and "The Balloon" deal with the textual surface of the sixties life, further revealing our cultural disposition to move in the direction of habitual forms. Barthelme knows his times like a sociologist, and records the effect of pressures which have led us to dependencies on advertising and mass-media sloganeering. In "Game" two air force missile crewmen stuck together for weeks in an underground silo devise their own cold war (over a game of jacks) comparable in subtlety and absurdity to what goes on above ground, among diplomats. A single Barthelme sentence can offer a solid clue to the pattern of contemporary life.

Snow White (New York: Atheneum, 1967) is Donald Barthelme's extended treatment of the sixties, using versions of the Grimms' and Disney's fairy tale as constants in this test of variables in a present-day story. The dwarfs suddenly become *a group,* from which one of the dwarfs *withdraws,* while the others speculate "that he doesn't want to be involved in human situations any more. A withdrawal. Withdrawal is one of the four modes of dealing with anxiety" (p. 4), and so forth through the litany of complaints (and jargon to describe them) which seem to exist only in the sixties. Snow White herself is bored. "Oh I wish there were some words in the world that were not the words I always hear!" she complains, trapped within the imag-

inative death that being a housewife implies (Barthelme further textualizes
the word by writing it as "horsewife"):

THE HORSEWIFE IN HISTORY

FAMOUS HORSEWIVES

THE HORSEWIFE: A SPIRITUAL PORTRAIT

THE HORSEWIFE: A CRITICAL STUDY

FIRST MOP, 4000 BC

VIEWS OF ST. AUGUSTINE

VIEWS OF THE VENERABLE BEDE

EMERSON ON THE AMERICAN HORSEWIFE

OXFORD COMPANION TO THE AMERICAN
HORSEWIFE

INTRODUCTION OF BON AMI, 1892

HORSEWIVES ON HORSEWIFERY

ACCEPT ROLE, PSYCHOLOGIST URGES

THE PLASTIC BAG

THE GARLIC PRESS (p. 61)

Snow White would like to complete herself, to imagine something better. But the contemporary world cannot offer her a prince, and the candidate who shows up turns out to be pure frog. The dwarfs themselves opt
out for "equanimity," and the fairy tale ends in a shambles. The characters
in it have been so defined by topical labels that they cannot act for real. Like
the Barthelme story that they are, they fall victim to arbitrary structures
they mistakenly perceive as real, an object lesson the sixties was to learn.

In 1970 poet Eve Merriam published a book titled *The Nixon Poems*
(New York: Atheneum) which, like this quality of Barthelme's work,
warned against the negative transformations that might be made when
others did our imagining for us. Her "Checklist" (p. 37) gives a rundown of
familiar terms—"authentic," "family," "living," and the like—together
with their actual usage in commercial culture. In this manner "authentic"

becomes "a reproduction, as in 'an authentic reproduction of early American.'" By the same token, "fresh" means "frozen," as in "fresh-frozen orange juice." Families of cars or food products, "honest" unmentholated cigarettes—Merriam shows how the abuses of language have created a new, counterfeit reality, which we nonetheless live by as if it were the real Mc-Coy. The virtue of Vonnegut's and Barthelme's fiction is that it uses the same contemporary principle to save language, to save fiction, and to save our abilities to imagine other worlds, so that the world we actually live in can be made a better place.

CHAPTER FIVE

James Kunen, Dotson Rader, and Hunter S. Thompson: The Art of Protest

That the conditions of life could be materially and spiritually improved was one of the most distinctive beliefs of the sixties, and its expression—as protest against the established order—will be remembered along with the Vietnam War as one of the decade's most distinguishing factors. Other historical periods have had their disruptions, but this time elements and conditions were unique, because the American 1960s coincided with different phases of three significant protest movements: struggles for the rights of black citizens, women, and students.

The civil rights of black persons had been an issue since the planting of colonial Virgina, but the years from 1960 (date of the Greensboro, North Carolina lunch-counter sit-in) to 1964–1965 (when the Civil Rights and Voting Rights Acts were passed by Congress) brought the three-and-one-half century struggle to a pitch of intensity unwitnessed since the antebellum Abolitionist Movement and the Reconstruction Era. An emerging sense of personal identity, part of the sixties aesthetic to be discussed in Chapter Eight, enhanced this social struggle.

The sixties closed with the first stirrings of a nationally organized but popularly based movement demanding full civil and human rights for women. In its prime a component of the seventies, the equal rights movement at times described itself as a parallel to the black civil rights struggle. But because of its strong basis in the middle class it had and continues to have more in common with the collegiate protests of the later sixties, which challenged the mainstream American attitudes which had yet survived the changes wrought by efforts for racial equality.

Student activism, then, can be seen as the central protest movement of the decade, in the sense that it cued itself off an overlapping black activist decade of its own (from the *Brown vs. Board of Education* decision by the United States Supreme Court in 1954 to President Lyndon Johnson's endorsement of Dr. Martin Luther King's "We Shall Overcome") and paved the way for a wide range of more specific protests in the seventies. The protestors against the war, the draft, and collegiate authority were inspired to action by the example of a racial and economic minority, even though the protestors were largely white, middle-class youths destined to inherit the privileged status of their parents. The fact that they were young was important, for the early years of the sixties had reflected and worshipped a youth culture; what the young did now was front-page material, both for news and human interest.

More importantly, their protests were exercised with a sense of style, so much so that by the decade's end the last Yippie protests were made up of little else but style. Style is in fact the key to understanding the role of student protest in the sixties. Older political activists who tried to join found that their 100 percent approval of the movement's goals could not alone buy them membership in it; if they did not respond to the new style which was emerging, they found themselves hopelessly out of step.

James Kunen, Dotson Rader, and Hunter S. Thompson are three professional journalists who were in their teens (or in Thompson's case, twenties) during the sixties. Kunen and Rader were students at Columbia during the 1968 disruptions and wrote their first books closely after the events. Thompson joined the fray earlier, covering the Berkeley Free-Speech Movement demonstrations in 1965 and keeping close to virtually every subsequent event in the counterculture for the next decade. What links them together is not so much their common subject matter as their approach to it. In all three cases, the result of their writing is not a compilation of facts but rather a style of arranging them—and a unique way of confronting them— which makes their books less historical achievements than artistic ones. Kunen, Rader, and Thompson are at the far edge of a developing genre, the New Journalism, and as the more established New Journalists imitate the mode of conventional novelists, these younger experimentalists show strong resemblances to the innovative fictionists of their same day.

For Kunen, Rader, and Thompson, the object of protest is only the beginning of their story. Like other New Journalists, they identify the action mainly so they can put themselves at the center of it. Once there, they write with honesty and authority (no illusions, they agree with the innovative fictionists) about themselves. Object therefore yields to response, but only temporarily. Before their books are done, each must be molded into a true work of art. Writing about student protests in the sixties compounds that necessity, for the writer must devise a new shape or form to capture the way new meanings are conveyed. Columbia-1968 simply cannot be described in the style of Panty-Raid-1958 or We-Shall-Overcome-1964, though there are elements of both to consider. Moreover, if one is to be a center of personal reactions and a writer at the same time, the resulting product must be valid as art to be useful or meaningful for anyone else.

Identifying the true object of protest can be difficult enough, when the protestors are asking for nothing less than a new order of values, a new reality. That such information was not automatically available to older working journalists, even to such an artistic professional as Norman Mailer who had understood John Kennedy's heroic image at the decade's start, can be seen from Mailer's own confusion in his coverage of the October 1967 march against the Pentagon, *Armies of the Night* (New York: New American Library, 1968). Throughout the action Mailer finds it impossible to describe the protest in its own relevant terms; the illustrations and comparisons he chooses inevitably involve his combat experience in World War II, images from the Civil War, football, or distant memories of adolescent rowdiness. Although he had relished John Kennedy's promise of change, in these more practically combative circumstances Mailer stands for order— he cannot tolerate the loose discipline of the young marchers. And he stands for logic—that the march has no definable goal deeply irritates him. The Pentagon itself is a symbol, and he found himself in the unlikely role of "marching not to capture it, but to wound it *symbolically;* the forces defending that bastion reacted as if a symbolic wound could prove as mortal as any other combative rent" (p. 54). The only style he perceived in the event was comic, particularly for the ground rules drawn up by a joint committee of protestors and government officials.

> The compromise said in effect: we, the government, wage the war in Vietnam for our security, but will permit your protest provided it is only a little disorderly. The demonstrators: we still consider the war outrageous and will therefore break the law, but not by very much. (p. 240)

Finally, his own role could be visualized only in the most abstract terms. Mailer and his participating contemporaries (especially poet Robert Lowell and critic Dwight Macdonald) struggled to be in the march's vanguard and among the very first arrested, since "That seemed the best way to satisfy present demands and still get back to New York in time for their dinners, parties, weekend parts" (p. 118). The insights in *Armies of the Night* come only after Mailer's reasonable plan has been demolished by the irrationalities of the government and its law enforcement agencies—absurdities to which the younger protestors were already responding in their own characterization of the march.

James Kunen has a better sense of the decade's irrationalities. He understands that they are basically a matter of fractured style, as Joseph Heller expressed it in the syntax of *Catch-22,* and that they pervade all aspects of his life, both as civilian and as combatant. He considers how strange it is that no one goes to jail for waging wars or for advocating them, but that prisons are being filled with war resisters. At the same time, he can walk down the street in his student neighborhood and find a store advertising itself as "Hard to Get Records" and wonder if they have easy-to-get records too. They must, for if they didn't, that would make them hard to get, and hence the store would have them.

Kunen sails on the crest of such logic, using it to improvise an exhilarating gamesmanship, rather than being tied by frustrations like the older Mailer. He can counter the abuses of the new reality on its own terms. Dotson Rader can take part in street demonstrations that seem more theatrical and romantic than tactically functional, because he knows the real issue is creating space for the hoot-and-holler expression of young manhood which has been uniquely repressed by the smooth society. And Hunter S. Thompson, facing the equally trying experiences of riding with the Hell's Angels, Richard Nixon, and the denizens of Las Vegas, admits that the only way to handle the absurdities which pass for reality is to match them with ridiculous creations of one's own. Las Vegas, for example, provides so many images of the extreme that even Thompson is hard pressed to exceed it. But he does not give up. Instead, like Kunen, he realizes that the situation has endowed him with a perfect opportunity to improvise: "The only hope now, I felt, was the possibility that we'd gone to such excess, with our gig, that nobody in a position to bring the hammer down on us could possibly *believe* it." Being confronted with a twisted reality is only a challenge to twist it farther, and the personal act of twisting allows one to legitimize one's coverage of the subject by taking part in it. Kunen, Rader, and Thompson become their subjects, while Mailer tries to remain the objective observer, the very stance which promises to keep him from perceiving the new world at hand.

Kunen's first book, *The Strawberry Statement* (New York: Random House, 1969), traces the history of Columbia's protests to a similar challenge of official logic: Mark Rudd's complaint that the university president's eulogy for Dr. Martin Luther King was hypocritical while the school persisted in paying black maids unfairly low wages and raking in profits as New York's largest slumlord. Kunen accepts the symbolic nature of much of the students' protest (laboriously barricading one gate while seven others remain open) because he knows how much of his very real life is based on symbolic propositions. *The Strawberry Statement* is subtitled "Notes of a College Revolutionary"; Kunen's next book, *Standard Operating Procedure* (New York: Avon, 1971), written as a framework for Vietnam war-crimes testimony, bears the subtitle "Notes of a Draft-age American," and offers good examples of just such symbolic power. One soldier, whose testimony Kunen hears, explains how he was drafted. "I didn't want to go, I didn't want to leave a girl, a family, a year of college, but I had mononucleosis, I was in the hospital, had to drop out to save my grade index. I missed the refund date for my money by five days," he reports, "therefore I was broke, had to gain fifteen hours within three months, work full time and pay for that fifteen hours while I was doing full-time study, and make enough money to get right back in again to keep from being drafted after completing that fifteen. And I'm not that type of student," he concludes. "Therefore I got drafted" (p. 115). Such technicalities, and their real-life impact, are beyond Mailer's experience, but for Kunen's generation they were a way of life. And so as a writer he must shape his response in the form of their reality.

As for describing the action, "Our whole Vietnam vocabulary is a lexicon of distortion," Kunen discovers, and so feels no compulsion to use rational methods to describe an irrational subject. South Vietnam should always be referred to as the Republic of Vietnam, the Military Assistance Command tells reporters, while the Democratic Republic of Vietnam must conversely be called North Vietnam; the twisted logic reflects the reality of their intentions. As for actual operations, they are clouded in technologies beyond the fears of George Orwell—"cross-cultural empathy facility, indigenous Vietnamese personnel, retrospective plausibility basis, VC infrastructure detail, laterally disseminated on a discretionary basis," and so forth. "Realtime online computer-controllrd wish evaporation," as Donald Barthelme would say. The language means nothing because the action is essentially meaningless, as the pointless pursuit of the Vietnam war eventually proved. "Destroying a village in order to save it" becomes a valid expression of the self-cancelling logic by which the war was fought. Beneath it all, Kunen perceives a goal:

> Body count, gross national product, batting average, weapons captured, percentage unemployed, goals and assists, earned-run average, tons of supplies destroyed, official times at bat, wholesale-price index, bases stolen, Industrial Average, defection rates, RBIs, slugging percentage, passing completion average, cost-of-living index, crime rate, hamlet-pacification rating, fielding average, industrial output, free-throw average, kill ratio—it's all the same, all an attempt to get a handle on the world with numbers, and thus make it manageable. (p. 25)

But the manageability is a chimera, for the language has only made the subject disappear. Kunen finds that in human experience, one thousand times apples equals one thousand apples, while one thousand times human beings equals one thousand. Faced with the death of Robert Kennedy in *The Strawberry Statement,* Kunen is at a loss to understand it, for death is no longer absolute. The new times have made it a relative affair—sometimes light, sometimes heavy, sometimes moderate. And you are not shot at; "fire is directed at your position." There are no dead men, only body counts. Death, the one reality which might effectively challenge the war, no longer exists.

Above all, the new terms of power in society oppress the young. Only in the 1960s did students begin questioning their disenfranchisement in Constitutional terms, along the lines that issues as petty as dorm hours and dress codes were violations of their civil liberties. But personal freedom was a larger issue, understandable in comparative terms if authority was made to answer why one class of young adults should be singled out for discriminatory treatment. That colleges would limit personal freedom, students learned, was part of the same mind-set which also denied them a voice in determining their curriculum. The next step was realizing that college authorities who dictated personal and curricular rules behaved this same way in their dealings with the outside world, including real estate and investment holdings (which, as in Columbia's case, tended to exploit minorities) and encouragements to broaden the war (through Defense Department and CIA connections). College-based protests, then, were neither frivolous nor conveniently occasional. Students were responding with a heightened awareness to a whole new set of values, which followed in the logical chain from their college administrators to the power structure of society. They were merely attacking the closest target, the one which most immediately affected their lives.

The most personal connection between state power and personal manhood is made by Dotson Rader, a Columbia senior in 1968 (Kunen was a sophomore) who quickly wrote a trilogy of the movement's rise and fall: *I Ain't Marchin' Anymore* (New York: David McKay, 1969), *Gov't Inspected Meat* (New York: David McKay, 1971), and *Blood Dues* (New York: Alfred A. Knopf, 1973). He finds the beginning in a group of young Americans who take the idealism of the country's founding for real. "It *was* to have been such a different place," he writes in his first book. "That is what we loved about it. Its former promise. But then I was going to be so different, too. I was going to try to make the world a better place to live in" (p. 3). His demand is that the American Dream be realized, "And it was this demand—that a national abstraction be actualized—which made us quintessentially American" (p. 8). The quest is personally real because existence is threatened; there is nothing theoretical about his challenge, it is a desperate struggle for life.

Young middle-class whites, Rader argues, were in the unique position of having to create personhood for themselves while "finding relief from tribal guilt, guilt whose victims clutter the ghettos of urban America. For them redemption is in rebellion" (p. 39). To injure that emerging sense of personhood, whether one be a university dean or a draft-board secretary, was a serious business indeed. For the protestors, mounting resistance to such challenges gave them the first sense of true effectiveness they had ever been able to feel, given the state of prolonged adolescence in which college and the draft had kept them well into their twenties. Why the demonstrations, the massing of bodies in college quadrangles and Pentagon driveways? "We wanted a response *to us*. Any kind . . . we could no longer tolerate being disregarded." In a country whose system emasculates young men, Rader argues, "street disorders, seizures of buildings, dislocation, confrontation, the tempting of violence had become rituals of manhood" (p. 174). The abstractly symbolic behavior at the Pentagon, so foreign to Norman Mailer, was for Dotson Rader a very real occasion:

> Al, Sean and I played the mall, running from one side to the other, joining bands of young men who attempted occasional penetrations of the troop lines, shouting End The War! laughing, catching glimpses of McNamara and the Generals at the windows, raising our fingers in a V-salute, laughing. None of us had ever been at the Pentagon before. It made you high dancing on the grass, natant with the tension, the sheer joy of being where the military did not want you to be, running now and again when the troops, ordered by their superiors to amuse the watching Mr. McNamara with a show of force, would rush out boldly, awkwardly in little groups into the crowd and attempt to push the protestors back. (p. 67)

Of course the specific action is ridiculous. Dodging the cops on campus reminded James Kunen of a game of red light. But the protestors are being noticed, and can notice that they are being noticed, beyond any solid, rational goals. Formal political effectiveness is less important than the personal benefit, as Rader confesses:

> No matter what we did or did not do, nothing would have a determining effect on the political system. We simply did not exist politically anymore. Demonstrations had become a kind of theatre, a play through which we mollified our outrage. We were doing what we had to do outside of political actuality. Violence was wanted. I hungered for it. I wanted to fight in front of my chick. To prove myself. (p. 174)

Rader's second book, *Gov't Inspected Meat,* is written as a novel—to generalize the specifics of the Columbia protest, to show how the psychic reality of the times extends beyond the campus borders, and to give the author more latitude in responding to his subject. The narrator comes from a class of young males equally disenfranchised with their brothers in college: untrained, undereducated kids whom the technologized society has passed by. These same born losers form the membership base of the biker clubs Hunter Thompson describes in *Hell's Angels* (1967), but Rader prefers to cast them in a more suggestive role, as sexual street hustlers. Their sexuality is an expression, but a perverted one, a necessary exploitation in a world which recognizes only commercial values. America has let these boys down. On the personal level of his narrator, Rader characterizes the sense of loss in the figure of a failed father, who deserts his son both physically and spiritually. A thinly fictionalized Norman Mailer (called "Sam Parsons") takes over the role of failed-father figure, once the action has progressed from back-home Evanston to big-time New York. Parsons understands this young man no better than Mailer can figure out Rader and his crowd at the Pentagon.

The real Norman Mailer appears in Rader's *Blood Dues,* again anxious to participate but hopelessly out of step. Sexuality is the real reason. For Mailer its natural expression is sinful, dirty, and lust-filled; in *Armies of the Night* he quarrels with Paul Goodman over that writer's opposite approach. For Rader, sex is dirty only when society has perverted it; the sad fact is that the perversity runs so deep that dirtiness is all that is left. "It was difficult to posit manhood in America," he writes early on, "for the values that corporate capitalism intruded into the culture and the social institutions it created were antihuman and antisexual. They were perverse" (p. 8). Mailer called this function the Corporation. Ken Kesey used another term, the Combine. But only Rader's generation was able to fashion a lifestyle in resistance to it, building new energy centers to replace those denied to them.

Of course, such improvisation with made-up alternatives could lead to a topsy-turvy life, and Rader is the first to admit it. In *Blood Dues,* his study of why the movement disintegrated after 1970, he compared the excitement over new social issues to a drug rush. "Its ambitions remained constant (the will to power, like a sexual drive, is constant in its passion), while its immediate objectives shifted constantly. It had to be reinvented every morning." Hence the helter-skelter dash from one cause to another:

> Someone was always coming along with a new line or cause or political fashion, and like a meth spike shoved in an adolescent arm, these new intrusions of concern and ideology acted on the movement the way speed does on the body. They gave a temporary rush, an energy high, and ended leaving the subject more debilitated and divided and fatigued and disoriented than before. (pp. 106–107)

The unfortunate result was that "It produced instability, if that word can be politically defined as the incapacity to establish lasting priorities." But a fact of life in the sixties was that no stable definition of value could long sustain itself, for the establishment simply had too much power—and that power was derived from the *Catch-22* antilogic of its working philosophy. The only alternative was to refashion a life of pure process—exhilarating in art, but chaotic in organized politics:

> One was continually embracing and then abandoning modes of belief in light of new evidence or new demands or new situations resulting from a change in consciousness on the part of one radical constituency or another. One was continually out of step. (p. 107)

The constant attempt to redefine and reinvent ended for many in a riot of confusion. The lesson which Mailer did not learn, and which was clear to Rader only when he had experienced the movement's political failure, was that their definitions had been too strictly bound within the establishment's terms.

James Kunen and especially Hunter Thompson transcend those terms almost completely. Kunen will let himself be defined by radical politics no sooner than he would let the state control his feelings. Hence he keeps his place on the varsity crew throughout the Columbia disruptions, rowing in the afternoon and occupying the president's office at night. A conventional contradiction makes sound personal sense. In his *Fear and Loathing in Las Vegas* (New York: Random House, 1972) Thompson agrees that the political movements of the sixties cannot be analyzed in conventional terms. If so, the verdict would be total failure:

> Tim Leary a prisoner of Eldridge Cleaver in Algeria, Bob Dylan clipping coupons in Greenwich Village, both Kennedys murdered by mutants, Owsley folding napkins on Terminal Island, and finally Cassius/Ali belted incredibly off his pedestal by a human hamburger, a man on the verge of death. Joe Frazier, like Nixon, had finally prevailed for reasons that people like me refused to understand—at least out loud. (pp. 22–23)

The cultural construct of the sixties had to be reckoned with in completely different terms if it were to be a success, or make any sense at all.

For one, the supposed values of straight society, masquerading as level responsibility, must be revealed for the utter shams they are. Thompson is a genius at this, and his Las Vegas trip is a two-week romp among the symbols of the Good Life in corporate America. He examines the casino life and assorted side attractions, judging them to be twisted beyond the most lethal drug experience. He makes a collage of newspaper items relating to drug abuse in official places, including the Army. And he manipulates such procedures as rent-a-car insurance policies and bogus credit-card sheets to run up an outrageous hotel bill and utterly destroy two expensive automobiles, all the while maintaining his pose of authority-in-the-know ("I tried to put the top up, for privacy, but something was wrong with the motor. The generator light had been on, fiery red, ever since I'd driven the thing into Lake Mead on a water test"). Thompson knows no one will stop him, because he is *insured*—for two dollars per day he has purchased the right to run amok in one of the most expensive cities in America. No one will object, for their share of the profits is protected. "All I had to do was call the VIP agency and have another one delivered . . . maybe threaten them with a lawsuit because all four tires had exploded on me, while driving in heavy traffic. Demand an Eldorado, next time with four Michelin Xs. and put it all on the card . . . charge it to the St. Louis Browns" (pp. 196, 154).

Thompson's reasons for being in Las Vegas are themselves an example of corporate-blessed absurdity, which he is anxious to expose and exploit. His first assignment is to cover a dirt-bike race for *Sports Illustrated.* But the bikes run in separate heats against a stopwatch, not each other, and even the single bikes are lost in clouds of dust. There is nothing to see, let alone report. Following that, Thompson is asked by another magazine to file stories on a law-enforcement/drug-abuse convention, which he finds so hopelessly naive and misinformed that he is driven to perform the most heinous abuses right under their noses.

Fear and Loathing on the Campaign Trail '72 (San Francisco: Straight Arrow Books, 1973) is Thompson's coverage of the full presidential campaign, from the first primaries to the election wrap-up. Again, he was appalled by phoniness parading as truth. A liberal Democrat, he might be expected to have the meanest feelings about Richard Nixon, but his deepest revulsion was for Hubert Humphrey. Reviewing the case of "The Happy Warrior," Thompson complained,

> There is no way to grasp what a shallow, contemptible, and hopelessly dishonest hack old Hubert Humphrey really is until you've followed him around for a while on the campaign trail. The double-standard realities of campaign journalism, however, make it difficult for even the best of the "straight/objective" reporters to write what they actually think and feel about a candidate. (p. 209)

Therefore, Thompson swears to counter the pap of establishment journalism with such sentences as "Hubert Humphrey is a treacherous, gutless old ward-heeler who should be put in a goddamn bottle and sent out with the Japanese Current'' (a line picked up and quoted by *Newsweek*), and ''They don't hardly make 'em like Hubert any more—but just to be on the safe side, he should be castrated anyway'' (pp. 135, 259). Edmund Muskie fares only a little better, as a meeting with him is compared to being locked in a rolling boxcar with a vicious two-hundred pound water rat. Mayor Richard Daley is described as looking like a potato with mange. No other campaign reportage boasts such colorful and bizarre images—pictures which in the wake of Watergate confirm our worst suspicions about big-time politics.

With such writing Thompson is doing more than covering the campaign (à la Theodore H. White), more even than Norman Mailer's indicting of the several Republican National Conventions covered in *Some Honorable Men*. He is shaping his responses into a work of innovative art. In that most personally human testament can be found an interpretation of the new reality that sixties politics became. His strikingly violent images mean less in a conventional literary sense, where they would lead to a directly perceived meaning (think of the imagery and symbolism in traditional fiction—Hemingway's wounded veterans, Fitzgerald's blasted paradises). Instead, they work more in the manner of innovative fiction, where the expressive gesture of the artist (in this case a violently felt choice of imagery) exists primarily to show us the track of the artist's hand, the path of his emotions. James Kunen incorporates such gestures in the structure of his books, whose catch-as-catch-can organization is their most appealing feature. Dotson Rader is adept at this technique when he traces the romanticism present in virtually every student-revolutionary act—not by telling us so, but by drawing scenes where he himself gushes ecstatically about the lovely dark lawns of Columbia at night, the pollution and tear gas misting against the lamplights.

Both Kunen and Thompson make the writing of their books an integral part of the final product. Kunen writes four introductions and publishes each draft, and much of his diary-entry form serves as a narrative of the writing process itself. He warns the reader not to study his book in careful, linear fashion, for that is not how it was written, nor how it was first experienced. Thompson likewise works for a sense of personal (not historical) realism. Deadline pressure is part of the story, and the circumstances which drive him to hysteria are an important part of his subject. The book and his experience of writing it are living, human things. At times he abandons conventional chapter forms for unedited notes and tape-recorder transcriptions, and even then keeps distractions on the tapes (sounds of Secret Service helicopters buzzing the hotel) and so he will remember just how bad things were. As the antithesis of the conventional, responsible journalist, he will even lie, but in those falsehoods are a deeper strain of truth, as the country found out in the post-Watergate seventies:

> The President was not immediately available for comment on how he planned to spend his forty-five Big Ones, but Stans said he planned to safeguard the funds personally.
> At that point, McGregor cracked Stans upside the head with a Gideon Bible and called him a "thieving little fart." McGregor then began shoving the rest of us out of the room, but when Stans tried to leave, McGregor grabbed him by the neck and jerked him back inside. Then he slammed the door and threw the bolt . . .
> Jesus, why do I write things like that? I must be getting sick, or maybe just tired of writing about these greasy Rotarian bastards. (p. 349)

That techniques of innovative fiction should invade the provinces of mainstream news reporting is a signal of imaginative change in the world of art, but that such techniques should end up providing a more truthful picture than supposed standards of objectivity proves that the culture at large was forming a new interpretation of reality. The route protest took in the late sixties reflected this change, both in its political goals and the books written about its activities. The early protests were deadly serious, and the books about them, by students such as Mark Gerzon and Richard Zorza, made solemn, conventional reading. But the true nature of student protest emerged only in the more innovative works of James Kunen and Dotson Rader, who realized that the style of protest was often more important, and more effective, than the content. They shaped their books to reflect this new interest. Finally, Hunter Thompson cast himself as a guerrilla fighter inside the bastions of state capitalism, living within the enemy's stronghold and actually prospering by his improvision with its own rules, but undermining them all the same.

The last organized protests, and the last books written about them, were the work of such street-theater artists as Jerry Rubin and Abbie Hoffman, where the acts were pure symbol, and the writing pure parody. If such outrageous calls had been sounded at the beginning of the sixties, in protest's first days, no one would have followed, certainly not the sons and daughters of conventional middle-class Americans. But those white middle-class kids had already begun demonstrating, and the process took them through the stages of content, style, and parody, until by 1970 a virtually new life style existed for them, created right within the growing center of a new America.

CHAPTER SIX

Vietnam

Disruption and transformation characterize the sixties—in literature, music, art, politics, and even in the closely worked tactics of military science. Vietnam changed the Army, and warfare in general, no less radically than political disruptions altered the social reality of America itself.

The coincidence of American reaction to the war in Vietnam with a decade of profound cultural change at home was in fact no accident at all. The one reinforced the other, since the causes and consequences of each were similar. Khe Sanh and Woodstock, the Tet Offensive and the politics of riot and assassination, the One-hundred-first Airborne and the Jimi Hendrix Experience shared the same transformative energy. In 1960 all of them would have been incomprehensible; by 1968 they were the order of the day. And by the next year, with the decade's end, transformed reality was at hand. As Michael Herr concludes in his collection of Vietnam reports, *Dispatches* (New York: Knopf, 1977), "The year [1968] had been so hot that I think it shorted out the whole decade, what followed was mutation some kind of awful 1969-X" (p. 259).

Nor was the war in Vietnam a distant experience. Virtually every day of it was protested at home, in disruptions whose violence approached that of the war itself. The several marches on Washington, where hundreds of thousands filled the streets, may have been symbolic affairs. But Berkeley-1965, Madison-1967, and finally Kent State-1970 could be considered legitimate skirmishes and battles of the Vietnam War, complete with guerrilla forces (the students), government troops (the National Guard), and a small but unnerving list of casualties. Most decisively, Vietnam was felt to be an experience changing the very core of American life, reversing long-held values and leading to a new definition of heroism and the good human life.

The Vietnam War itself was as different from previous military conflicts as was *Slaughterhouse-Five* from *The Naked and the Dead,* the Beatles and Rolling Stones from the Four Freshmen, or the cartoons on *Sesame Street* from Mickey Mouse. Throughout the fifties future warfare was anticipated as Armageddon, and our military leaders were preparing for atomic conflict, not the guerrilla tactics of a long-term peasant/agrarian struggle which they confronted in Vietnam. When the war began, new strategies were needed to fight it, new techniques to describe it, and a new mentality to understand it. In Western experience dating back to the French colonialization in 1873, Indo-China had been the test for Promethean aspirations. In 1930, anticipating the political and philosophical change France would experience two decades later with the loss of her foreign holdings, André Malraux described the fictional adventurer Perken in *La Voie royale* (*The Royal Way*), a novel which parallels the failure of economic exploitation with the inadequacy of a male-dominant approach to sex. "Without love there can be no possession," Malraux wrote, signalling the end of a psychological as well as political age.

Graham Greene's novel of 1955, *The Quiet American,* was published just a year after France's defeat at Dien Bien Phu, and anticipates two decades of American blunders in Vietnam. Colonialization and adventuring now yield to a more subtly Promethean enterprise, the Agency for International Development, AID, and behind it the more perverse anagram of the CIA. France had desired Vietnam's body; America wanted her soul, and from the eagerness of Greene's American official to the "winning-hearts-and-minds" strategy of the hot war a decade later runs the same style of deconceptualized language and intellectual fraud which characterizes any operation whose validity died with an earlier age. Perken's quest in *La Voie royale* and Pyle's in *The Quiet American* are the same: self-annihilation. A worn-out idea consuming itself in an apocalyptic fire is the only reasonable explanation for a war which defied reason itself.

But the very unreasonableness of that war was being reflected in the new terms of reality being tested out at home by an increasing number of Americans. True patriots were now those who resisted war; cowards followed orders. Soldiers who did enlist or submitted to the draft marched not toward linear objectives ("On to Berlin!") but in circular, inconclusive patrols. Their goal was not the war's end but the duration of three hundred and sixty-five days in the country, with daily operations punched in and out like a time clock. Operations were conducted high on grass to the tune of transitorized rock and roll; barracks yielded to apartments or hootches with black light and stereo. Enemies blended with friendlies. There was no front, and no heroes' welcome home for a job well done. Nothing from previous wars seemed to apply.

Because of the radically different nature of this war, both in its initial combat abroad and in the resistance to it at home, conventional modes of understanding were discarded by many as obsolete. That was the first theme announced by the earliest novels to come out of the Vietnam experience: how the rubrics of previous wars were inapplicable to the new experiment in "counter insurgency," and especially how the tacticians of World War II and Korea, whose twenty-year Regular Army enlistments carried them into the first years of Vietnam, were baffled and frustrated by the new terms of combat.

This challenge makes the novels written during America's active engagement in the war the most interesting. When both soldiers and civilians faced in each day's experience or television news the new reality of Vietnam, there could be no reliance on stereotypes: the war was a challenge to the imagination, a test of the mind's power to organize and interpret in some meaningful way. This period of aggressive imaginative involvement ran from 1961 to 1970. At the beginning, 3,200 American soldiers were sent to Vietnam by President John Kennedy as "advisors." Following the Gulf of Tonkin incident on August 4, 1964, President Lyndon Johnson steadily increased this number until the informal designation of their status could no longer apply, and by March 1965 Army regulars were establishing permanent bases at DaNang.

Domestic dissent reached its peak in 1967, but the first major publicized reversal came in the months following the Tet Offensive (January 31, 1968), culminating in Johnson's unwillingness to commit more than the half-million American troops already in Vietnam and his decision not to seek a second full presidential term (where the war would be a major issue). This first period of involvement, especially on the home front, ended in late April and May of 1970, with President Richard Nixon's invasion of Cambodia, the massive student protests against that act, and the Ohio National Guard's killing of four students at Kent State University. Almost at once the debate of the war, both pro and con, dissipated into a feeling of resignation and defeat. Public opinion polls, which in broad samplings of the population had never counted more than 25 percent firm opposition to the war, now registered dissent at just above 50 percent, but no longer was it expressed as violent protest. Instead, the mood was nightmarish, of being stuck in a hideous morass with little hope of easy exit.

This dark hour of the Vietnam experience, which dragged on in a maddening time stasis from summer 1970 to the spring of 1975 (when Saigon finally fell to the North Vietnamese), dampened most literary efforts to describe the war. Few books and plays and even fewer films treated the subject, since Vietnam was considered a dead issue even as one peace discussion after another failed and the war dragged on. Following the Paris Agreements of January 31, 1973, the last American fighting troops came home, but the national presence in Vietnam was maintained through civilian advisors and massive military aid, which of course remained targets for the Viet Cong and North Vietnamese Army. When Saigon did fall in April 1975, Americans received the news as a traumatic but wearily welcomed end. Startling accounts of Americans and South Vietnamese sympathizers mobbing the embassy roof for helicopter lifts to warships in the Gulf, of South Vietnamese pilots ditching their aircraft near the carriers and swimming to safety on board, of the helicopters themselves—expensive and complex symbols of the war's technology—being pushed over the side to make room for more airborne refugees, all these scenes dominated American television for days and were watched with intense interest. It was the dramatization of a national agony no book or film had yet been able to express. The inevitable had happened: America had lost her first war, and in so doing had come of age. Vietnam was over.

Within a year the country was ready for aesthetic explanations. The *Wall Street Journal* announced that eleven major motion pictures were in production, among them three films which would be critically important in each succeeding year's crop: *Coming Home* (1977), *The Deer Hunter* (1978), and *Apocalypse Now* (1979). But these works, because of their uninvolved status, are less insightful than the fiction which struggled with the idea of Vietnam as the experience itself was evolving. The aesthetic truth of the war is in the works conceived in the sixties, not the seventies (when subtle falsifications begin).

The typical Vietnam novel from the war's active phase is a struggle for form, an attempt to find a structure for this apparently structureless world. The very act of writing a novel becomes as much a combat experience as the acts of war it describes, and this reinforcement of content by form makes such literary works more interesting to read today. An early device used by David Halberstam in *One Very Hot Day* (Boston: Houghton Mifflin, 1967) is to describe the plight of an American advisor, combat veteran of World War II and Korea, who finds his twenty years of soldiering experience practically worthless in the new world of Vietnam. Captain Beaupre is the first American to face Malraux's jungle, the first to sense that "the heat was the enemy of all white men," and especially his own personal enemy, for his past decade in the peacetime Army has made him flabby and prone to sweat even when resting. But more distressing are the artificial limits put on his soldier's role:

> He wished the troops would go faster, would move it out, and he wished he were a real officer, someone who could give commands and then see them obeyed, who could send a patrol here and another there, could make the troops go fast, go slow, be brave, be strong; wished to be hated, to be feared, even to be loved, but to be an officer and in charge. (p. 155)

Instead, the South Vietnamese troops he advises disregard traditional discipline and treat their operations as recreational strolls in the jungle. The operations themselves seem maddeningly absurd, even to Beaupre, for they rarely have an objective. For each operation his troops are airlifted into an area which they patrol in ever-widening circles. Then they reverse field and slowly close the circle, until the choppers come to carry them back to their comfortable urban barracks. Beaupre complains to his young, West Point-trained lieutenant:

> "We didn't know how simple it was, and how good we had it. Sure we walked, but in a straight line. Boom, Normandy beaches, and then you set off for Paris and Berlin. Just like that. No retracing, no goddam circles, just straight ahead. All you needed was a compass and good sense. But here you walk in a goddam circle, and then you go home, and then you go out the next day and wade through a circle, and then you go home and the next day you go out and reverse the circle you did the day before, erasing it. Every day the circles get bigger and emptier. Walk them one day, erase them the next. In France, you always knew where you were, how far you had walked, and how far you had to go. But this goddam place, Christ, if I knew how far I had walked, it would break my heart. From Normandy to Berlin and back, probably." (p. 114)

The absurd pattern of these circular patrols becomes Halberstam's structure for his novel; the character's search for meaning parallels the author's struggle for a form which might express the new reality of warfare in Vietnam. This earliest of the Vietnam novels starts with basics, a single day's patrol, but the point is that the veteran Captain even on this simplest of operations loses all sense of purpose and achievement. In elemental military terms, the Vietnam experience fails to make sense.

Structures to interpret the war figure prominently in *The Big V* (New York: Liveright, 1972), a novel written by combat veteran William Pelfrey during the war's active phase. Everything that happens resists identification with reality, since it first must be measured against the cliché warfare has become in a culture of stylized violence, whether in war movies, comics, or live combat coverage on TV. Pelfrey's characters never face the actual war because they form themselves into caricatures who role-play their way through stereotyped situations: John Wayne charging ashore at Iwo Jima, G. I. Joe taking out a German pillbox, or the battle-weary "grunts" mugging for the CBS News camera. Pop-art gestures are assigned to every act, all of which run through a whole catalogue of trite associations. As one character reports,

> I fired one round on semiautomatic. His body jerked erect, almost like a gangster blown back by a sawed-off shotgun, only screaming, hoarse, with his mouth gaping; more like an Indian, his arms flying up and dropping the rifle. (p. 36)

Pelfrey's narrator can find no vocabulary for the war beyond that of such popular-culture images because his own vision reaches no farther than the clichés of his childhood. The lesson? That Vietnam remained a mystification for so long because even the participants in it were blinded by their own stereotypes from an earlier, stereotypical aesthetic.

The better works from the war's hot phase recognize this dilemma and make it part of their own structural approach. In *The Weary Falcon* (Boston: Houghton Mifflin, 1971) Tom Mayer presents a correspondent describing "the US Marine landing at Chu Lai where the troops came storming out of the amtracks and up the beach like John Wayne in *The Sands of Iwo Jima* only to find twenty photographers on top of the first dune taking pictures of it all" (p. 95). And in *The Bamboo Bed* (New York: Simon & Schuster, 1969) William Eastlake employs the self-conscious Myth Americana which pervades the war to show how part of the confusion is due to the myth being reversed, in the case of an infantry captain who has led his men into a restaging of Custer's Last Stand:

> The grave-registration chopper came in low over the remains of Clancy's outfit. Everyone on Ridge Red Boy to Mike seemed very dead. They were quiet as lambs. Sometimes you could only see what looked like smoke coming up from a fire but it was only ground fog. Everyone with Clancy was dead. All the Alpha Company. It was the biggest thing since Custer. Mike, who called himself a correspondent, had to watch himself. You tended to take the side of the Indians. You got to remember that this is not the Little Big Horn. This is Vietnam. Vietnam. Vietnam. They all died in Vietnam. A long way from home. What were the Americans doing here? The same thing they were doing in Indian Country. In Sioux Territory. They were protecting Americans. They were protecting Americans from the Red Hordes. God help Clancy.
> You could tell here from above how Clancy blundered. Clancy blundered by being in Vietnam. That's a speech. The chopper circled now low over the dead battle. Clancy had blundered by not holding the ridge. Clancy had blundered by being forced into a valley, a declivity in the hills. It was the classic American blunder in Vietnam of giving the Indians the cover. The enemy was fighting from the protection of the jungle. You couldn't see them. Americans love the open. Americans do not trust the jungle. The first thing the Americans did in America was clear a forest and plant the cities. (pp. 24–25)

Eastlake is a skillful pioneer in the struggles of innovative fiction who encountered Vietnam by accident: a film production in Spain fell through, leaving him with a round-the-world plane ticket which he used to get to Vietnam and write a series of reports for *The Nation* magazine (subsequently collected in *A Child's Garden of Verses for the Revolution,* 1970).

He therefore finds it easy to adapt his language (note the singsong, shorthand-style sentences), characterization (Clancy as Custer), and plot (the inverse mythology whereby the Americans become the Redcoats while the Indians, or Minutemen so masquerading, become the Viet Cong) to the aesthetic situation in Vietnam, which reverses so many traditional values.

Vietnam did provide a new mythology, once authors' perspectives were broadened enough to appreciate it. Much of Dr. Ronald J. Glasser's *365 Days* (New York: Braziller, 1971) is devoted to vignettes of these new legends: of daredevil helicopter pilots, hotdogging first lieutenants, and above all the altruistic medics so devoted to their men that the Viet Cong can predict their behavior and drop them too. Another insight into the surprising way things really were comes from Josiah Bunting, an Army major and Vietnam veteran of combat command during the active war years, who uses the corporate structure of the modern Army as the plan for his own novel, *The Lionheads* (New York: Braziller, 1972). Bunting's revelation, to which more conventional eyes were blinded, was that the operations of MACV (Military Assistance Command, Vietnam) reflected less of Grant's Army of the Potomac or MacArthur's South Pacific command than it did of General Motors, IBM, or Coca-Cola International. For career officers, the Army means a managerial scramble for promotion, and the key to early promotion is a combat command. Bunting structures his novel on the Army chain of command, from Division down through Brigade to Company, Platoon, Squad, and the "Real Sharp Individual" the Army counts as the bottom line of its ledger, the foot soldier walking point on patrol. Bunting's chapters are so titled and follow this order from top to bottom. Up top are the generals who aspire to political rank. His general knows that

> commanding a Division in the combat theatre can be the capstone of an excellent career of service, leading to one further assignment . . . or, if he truly distinguishes himself, the assignment will lead to another promotion—the big step to three stars (only 15 percent of two-star generals are promoted to three-star rank). . . . He wants to be Chief of Staff—of the Army. (p. 15)

To win advancement, the general must produce results, and so he pressures his staff like a sales manager: move the product, build body counts. Among his three light colonels, each commanding a brigade, there is a scramble for success and the tools required—in this case "helicopter assets" which are inadequate for the whole division. One Brigade will inevitably be shorted, and will suffer heavier casualties for it.

Casualities, we learn, make no human impression in this system save at the lowest level of the "real sharp individual" most likely to catch it in the head, heart, or limbs. That individual, from start to finish, is PFC Compella, an infantry soldier who at the novel's beginning has been temporarily assigned to Division Headquarters, where he holds the map pointer for an operations officer briefing Command on the planned activities. The officers, of course, ignore Compella as a human being, seeing only the tip of his pointer. His presence is as unreal as the deaths orchestrated by these same commanders. By the novel's end we have worked our way down the chain of command to Compella's squad, which is leading the attack planned in the earlier chapters. It is an attack designed with one thing in mind: not the vanquishing of the Viet Cong, but the making of an Army Chief of Staff. The inevitable logic of the book leads to Private Compella's death, an event totally absurd within any system except that of the Army's careerism in Vietnam. For an absurd war, Bunting has found an absurdist structure which makes a readable novel and an informative statement on the style of Vietnam.

Military structure from an enlisted man's point of view is the organizing factor in James Park Sloan's *War Games* (Boston: Houghton Mifflin, 1971). The narrator, as did Sloan himself, drops out of Harvard College to experience Vietnam—particularly to see if the war confirms either of his two theses for a novel about it, either that a timid hero would face "a character-molding experience" and with "a flash of insight" become a soldier and a man, or that a tough protagonist might encounter "genuine brutality and tragedy" and with a "flash of insight" discover his own hidden sensitivity (p. 4). Neither thesis proves correct or even possible in the absurdist world of Vietnam. The narrator finally structures his war experience (as Sloan structures his novel) around a single real and stable element: his service dental chart, for which he is systematically complaining about every third tooth so that his mouth has VA insurance for life.

As a Company clerk, Sloan's narrator learns how artificial the war is. Encouraged to produce results, he falsifies casualties and invents a monthly battle to be placed on his map at random:

> I have standardized the statistics as well. Ours. Theirs. We lead by a steady three-to-one. Which is good, but not good enough. Any worse and there would be alarm. Any better and the statistics would be checked. No one really reads the reports. I never bother with the facts. When a town comes up on my roster, I put the monthly battle there. That's the way it is with this war. (p. 87)

He is soon adopted as the protégé of a Nietzschean colonel who agrees that in the sixties war is a matter of one's own invention. "Devise the play, then act in it!" (p. 9) the narrator tells himself, to which the colonel adds, "War is no longer waged merely to achieve ends; it is waged as proof of its own possibility" (p. 144). The Vietnam war in Sloan's hands seems less a creation of the general than a fiction conceived by a sixties novelist such as Thomas Pynchon, whose theory of social entropy describes Sloan's Vietnam: "It was more and more complex, but in the process its energy was spent" (p. 154).

The physical complexity of Vietnam, which with more and more action yielded increasingly less results, was in its weaponry. Line equipment included sophisticated aircraft and helicopters of all sizes, and command posts were often furnished with highly developed computers to devise combat strategy. If the gasses, machine guns, and tanks of World War I were the birth of modern technological warfare, Vietnam was the introduction to military postmodernism, a theme which figures in the best novel to come from the war's experience. William Crawford Woods, a Signal Corps veteran (1966–68) and professional writer, sets his novel *The Killing Zone* (New York: Harper's Magazine Press, 1970) in a New Jersey training camp where young soldiers are preparing for Vietnam. Virtually every theme and technique of Vietnam war literature is expressed in his book, including the coming-of-age-by-defeat thesis expressed by Ernest Hemingway's epigraph: "Do younger nations always win wars? They are apt to for a time. Then what happens? They become older nations." Another popular theme, that of the veteran sergeant finding himself out of touch with the new warfare and its young practitioners, gives the book its structure, for the action is played against the presence of the company's top-ranking Sergeant Melton, veteran of World War II and Korea, who by the death of his commander (heart attack on a golf course) becomes functioning executive officer until a replacement can be found.

During this time a young lieutenant arrives with a master's degree in information retrieval and a plan to computerize the moment-to-moment tactics of a line company in battle. Predictable ironies result. Melton had refused a battlefield commission in 1944, rejecting the managerial caste of the officers he so distrusted; now, in Lieutenant Track, he sees the absurd extreme of an officer who would technologize warfare with the methods of a fast-food operation. But Melton also feels alienated from both the trainees and their instructors, groups of young men barely three years apart in age but worlds apart in experience, for the instructors are young sergeants who have just survived a tour in Vietnam. These veterans in turn are distressed by the home-front ironies: of pizza trucks which stop for deliveries each night in the parking lot where by day the raw recruits learn to kill like cavemen, of leather-upholstered Corvettes, their built-in stereos blaring Rolling Stones music as the young lieutenants roar off for weekends in New

York City, of the general lack of seriousness as all of them go about their training exercises.

Lieutenant Track's computer exercise is a war game; with blank ammunition and fake artillery the company will go through the paces of an assault planned and executed by the computer. Sergeant Melton half-heartedly agrees, and Sergeant Cox and his instructor-colleagues skeptically lead their trainee-platoons into mock action. But as Cox's men charge a machine-gun nest, the impossible becomes actual (the pattern for Vietnam): man after man is cut down by real bullets, and not even the computer can help them reach the gunners to stop their unintended slaughter. The fault is a programming error: the operator has forgotten to routinely clear the computer's storage, and two boxes of live ammunition from a previous target practice session have found their way among the rounds of plastic-headed dummy bullets. The only prerogative, the last hope, belongs to the common foot soldier, Sergeant Cox, who has just one way to save his men:

> He had been hit four times by the gunner who was still firing when he reached him. Mr. Track's computer had provided an unbeatable realism which had gone into his belly, and one bit of realism had ruined his left arm, taken it out altogether. So it was with the rifle in one hand that he came over the barrel, calmly, indifferently, almost sweetly, and with practiced smoothness and precision slid the bayonet into the boy's chest, up to the hilt, not seeing the frightened and finally knowing glance down at the explosion of blood as cloth and skin and muscle and then bone gave way to the rushing pouring steel. Cox's finger jerked on the trigger and a short stream of plastic bullets squirted into the open wound, spashing hot into the welling lake of blood. The sergeant and private fell together behind the finally silent gun. (p. 164)

Sergeant Cox has attacked the one real enemy in the Vietnam War: technology itself, which removes the human will from killing and then effaces the human reality of death, which in Vietnam created not only a military machine but an Orwellian language of obfuscation in order to drive all sense from its operation. But because he searches out and destroys this enemy, Cox proves both himself and the true manner of death, something others thought impossible in the sixties. *The Killing Zone* affirms just what remains of honor, and describes the obstacles that sense of honor faces. The villains are those who disavow such human behavior, whether they be technocrat lieutenants who fight weekday wars while spending weekends in the city or an establishment which has lost sight of the purpose of soldiering, the saddest casualty of Vietnam.

A legacy of Vietnam, which carried over into the Watergate years of the seventies, was a tendency on the part of authority toward Orwellian language—fancy, Latinate constructions which in their disregard of Anglo-Saxon hard sense helped obscure the insane rhetoric beneath. As James Kunen has noted, enemy soldiers were no longer killed; fire was directed at their position. And death itself was not absolute, since casualities could be described as "moderate" or "light." The unmentionable term "genocide" was replaced by the technocratic "free fire zone"; enemy areas, particularly homes, were not destroyed but "pacified"; the round-the-clock bombing of North Vietnam, surpassing in tonnage all previous wars put together, was sporadically interrupted by "bombing pauses," which were part of what President Johnson's administration called "peace initiatives." The effacement of reality by language becomes a minor theme in the film *Apocalypse Now,* when the renegade Colonel Kurtz is targeted for the Special Forces captain, not *to be killed* (in so many words) but to be "terminated with extreme prejudice," a deceitful way of saying the same thing.

If novelists faced a problem with structure, journalists faced the problem of simple truth, and as the Vietnam war progressed more and more correspondents were relieved of their credentials as their stories won credibility among dissenters to the war. One reporter, whose first pieces appeared in *Esquire* (the sponsoring journal) and in *Rolling Stone* (the archetypal paper of disaccredited journalists), was Michael Herr, whose collection *Dispatches* was not published until 1977, long after the hot war had fizzled out, even though several of its sections were written in the sixties.

"I went to cover the war," Herr begins, "and the war covered me"—the signal experience which in turn became the methodology of the New Journalism. "You were as responsible for everything you saw as for everything you did," he adds, making his new style of reporting especially pertinent to the irresponsible mess of Vietnam:

> The problem was that you didn't always know what you were seeing until later, maybe years later, that a lot of it never made it in at all, it just stayed stored there in your eyes. Time and information, rock and roll, life itself, the information isn't frozen, you are. (p. 20)

The event which freed Michael Herr's imagination to complete his book was the fall of Saigon, specifically the chopper ditchings displayed so dramatically on TV. "The war ended," Herr reports, "and then it really ended, the cities 'fell,' I watched the choppers I'd loved dropping into the South China Sea as their Vietnamese pilots jumped clear, and one last chopper revved it up, lifted off and flew out of my chest" (pp. 259–260).

Herr's own imaginative life has been one with Vietnam's, and the value of *Dispatches* is that through its style of language and pacing of events it recreates the war's spiritual truth. He describes the book's process as

"Years of thinking this or that about what happens to you when you pursue
a fantasy until it becomes experience, and then afterward you can't handle
the experience until I felt I was just a dancer too" (p. 68). Most of the
fantasies-become-truth of the Vietnam war, which by their very unconven-
tionality had no choice but to become fantasies again, are represented in
Dispatches. Rock and roll in one ear and machine-gun fire in the other;
technology for the sake of its own motion; a war without goals or even
patterns—all the staples of Vietnam era fiction are here as fact. So too is the
language, abstracted into emptiness by the military politicians and restored
to life by the infantry "grunts." "It seemed the least of the war's contradictions," Herr discovered, "that to lose your worst sense of American shame
you had to leave the Dial Soapers in Saigon and a hundred headquarters
who spoke goodworks and killed nobody themselves, and go out to the
grungy men in the jungle who talked bloody murder and killed people all
the time" (p. 42). Herr seeks out the reality at the front and, by implication,
at home, where "rock stars started falling like second lieutenants" (p. 258).
His deepest scorn is for the conventional press, which "never found a way
to report meaningfully about death" in such circumstances, "which of
course was really what it was all about" (p. 215). "Conventional journalism
could no more reveal this war than conventional firepower could win it" (p.
218).

Hence *Dispatches* violates every convention of war reporting. Except
for the seige of Khe Sanh and the destruction of Hue ("Looks like the Im-
perial City's had the schnitz," a Marine tells Herr on page 76), events which
Americans could follow in the news, we never know where we are. Nor is
there a clear focus on the fighting, only the reactions of author and friends,
for the GIs have become Herr's buddies. The truth conveyed is of the
author's experience, and that experience defies the stereotypes of previous
wars. His prose conveys the rhythms of the action and the absurd logicality
which made the war so crazy:

> "If you get hit," a medic told me, "we can chopper you back to a
> base-camp hospital in like twenty minutes."
> "If you get hit real bad," a corpsman said, "they'll get your case
> to Japan in twelve hours."
> "If you get killed," a spec 4 from Graves promised, "we'll have
> you home in a week." (p. 21)

In a long paragraph on page 134, the ways of getting hit are described in a
staccato symphony of either/or clauses, eclipsing the rules of warfare and
the fields of honor so thoroughly that simply to be on the Vietnamese earth
makes one's life a liability. By putting the reader through the physical paces

of such sentences, paragraphs, and dialogues, the imaginative experience of Vietnam is recreated and conveyed.

Because the dominant officialdom which prosecuted the war never shared this experience, Vietnam became the mutation most now admit it was. One last part of Herr's technique is to place the war within the Myth Americana so many fictionists pondered:

> Vietnam was where the Trail of Tears was headed all along, the turn-about point where it would touch and come back to form a containing perimeter; might just as well lay it on the proto-Gringos who found the New England woods too raw and empty for their peace and filled them up with their own imported devils. Maybe it was already over for us in Indo-China when Alden Pyle's body washed up under the bridge at Dakao, his lungs all full of mud; maybe it caved in with Dien Bien Phu. But the first happened in a novel, and while the second happened on the ground it happened to the French, and Washington gave it no more substance than if Graham Greene had made it up too. (p. 49)

It isn't Michael Herr's argument that the Myth Americana was reversed by Vietnam. Rather, the popular interpretation of that myth had been wrong for centuries until Vietnam revealed what it really was, another part of the coming-of-age thesis. "Re-visioning" man's experience, rethinking man's definition of himself, was the critical and philosphical style being suggested by Ihab Hassan during these same years, to be collected later in his *Paracriticisms* and *The Right Promethean Fire* (Urbana: University of Illinois Press, 1975 and 1980). That such reorganization of imaginative experience took place in the sixties under the impact of Vietnam and correlative domestic events is clear from the totally rethought pictures we get of World War II in Kurt Vonnegut's *Slaughterhouse-Five* (1969) and of the Korean conflict in Richard Hooker's *M.A.S.H.* (1968).

A contrary re-visioning of Vietnam itself has taken place in the films about the war conceived and produced in the late seventies, which have progressively falsified the war's true meaning. The first major and artistically significant treatment was *Coming Home* (1977), in which a careerist Marine captain's wife undergoes a change of experience and of values in the company of a disabled and pacifistic Vietnam vet while her husband is off finding his own disappointment in the war. Although a bit obvious in its manner of presentation, *Coming Home* is a fair approximation of sixties attitudes. But with *The Deer Hunter* (1978) the style begins to change, from rock music to modernist classics in the soundtrack and for more traditional styles of behavior and morality in its theme. Three steelworkers enlist for generally patriotic and adventuresome motives and are physically and psychologically mutilated by the war's horrors. But instead of seeking a correlative for the unexplainable in the nature of experience itself (Michael Herr's way), the creators of *The Deer Hunter* choose an all-too-easy and, to earlier generations, familiar answer: the inhumane beastliness of Oriental peoples (the "yellow peril" of the Pearl Harbor years). Not one Vietnamese character is presented as a human being; if Vietnam was a horror, this film says, it was because Orientals are horrible creatures and that's where the war took place.

The final regression to stereotypes occurs in *Apocalypse Now* (1979), where the nature of the Vietnam war (portrayed to the director's credit with some fidelity) is made the responsibility of an old nemesis, described long ago and again in this film by Joseph Conrad's *Heart of Darkness,* T. S. Eliot's *The Waste Land,* and by Eliot's sources, Jesse L. Weston's *From Ritual to Romance* and Sir James Frazer's *The Golden Bough* (noted in their paperback editions by the director's roving camera): the bestial heart of man.

To the late seventies, a decade removed from the hot war, Vietnam must be re-visioned as an adventure more like its own emotional experience, just as certain of the more aggressive features of the war have been refined in the popular memory as really not so drastic at all. But then each generation rewrites history in its own image, and the gross disparity between popular views of Vietnam as the seventies ended with the aesthetic struggle recorded by novelists and journalists more closely involved suggests again that the sixties were a quite distinct period with a remarkable contribution to be made to the ongoing progress of American culture, even as the following decade (like the thirties to the twenties) voiced its regrets.

CHAPTER SEVEN

Bob Dylan and Neil Young: The Song of Self

Positively Main Street, as Toby Thompson called his book about the young Mr. Dylan. Solid hometown roots, squarely within the American middle class, featuring comfortable homes with televisions, appliances (which his father sold for a living), and *Saturday Evening Post*s with covers by Norman Rockwell and stories by Kurt Vonnegut, Jr.—these are the elements of Bob Dylan's background, against which he posed a new imaginative life. The discoveries he made in Hibbing, Minnesota, during the late 1950s were shared by an entire generation and eventually by a whole culture. Late-night clear channel radio from Little Rock and Nashville, a music store equipped to fill special orders for blues records and harmonica racks, and a social environment which could be effectively challenged by a loud and iconoclastic high school rock band were not unique to Hibbing during these years, and while they may not have been the universal experiences of all American teenagers, seventies culture (through movies, television programs, and memories) has tended to mythologize the sixties decade this way.

What can be shown is how Bob Dylan found within this culture enough elements, positive and negative, to form his own artistic work for the 1960s. The genius of this work is that it choreographed a decade's progress, from the civil rights protests of the early sixties (Dylan sang at Dr. Martin Luther King's great assembly in Washington), through the youth culture's adoption of a fully alternative life-style in the decade's middle years, to the SDS/Weatherman "Days of Rage" in October, 1969, when a tag line of Dylan's "Subterranean Homesick Blues" gave a political movement both a name and background music for its coverage on network news.

Yet Bob Dylan's importance is far more than political. His growth through the sixties anticipated the general direction of popular music, from folk through hard rock to country. His albums *Freewheelin'* (1963), *Highway 61 Revisited* (1965), and *Nashville Skyline* (1969) are milestones in the popular culture, effectively predicting where larger musical trends would be in succeeding years. In the end, those styles gave shape to general attitudes which Dylan's music managed to express. Pressed to describe Bob

89

Dylan's importance in just a few words, music encyclopedist Lillian Roxon simply wrote, "he is a continuing autobiography of this country."

The gift of Bob Dylan is that he helped provide a new language for the emerging culture, a musical and poetic form drawn from previously overlooked or discarded elements of American life, which young people like himself found helpful to voice their personal and unique beliefs. Once established, more commercial groups such as the Beatles and the Rolling Stones built it into the major music of the day, but the first step was having individuals like Bob Dylan searching through all that was available to them, looking for an alternative to what their daily lives had to offer. The surface life of Hibbing, with songs by Patti Page, Perry Como, and Vaughn Monroe (and deeper cultural values to match) did not exist without an underside. After midnight, any teenager with a radio could tune in to WLAC in Nashville and hear John R. play records never meant for white, Northern ears, certainly not for young minds eager for new ideas and values. From Little Rock, Arkansas, the accidentals of 50,000 watt power and clear channel broadcasting gave Gatemouth Page an audience wildly beyond the advertising market his programming might reflect, which offered ointment, salves, home remedies, and mail-order items of interest to a listenership assumed to be Southern, rural, and black.

What Bob Dylan and millions of other teenage listeners heard was a "race-market" music not even distributed in the North: Bobby Blue Bland, James Brown, Jimmy Reed, Fats Domino, Little Richard, the early Chuck Berry, and even comedy by Moms Mabley and Pigmeat Markham, adding up to styles and attitudes far from the white, middle-class world these kids lived in by day. But there were also strong stimuli coming from the daytime world, not all negative, and from this combination of resources was built an attitude which would carry Dylan and his generation into the new decade, when even Moms and Pigmeat would find themselves on nationwide TV as integral parts of a whole new cultural style. Bob Dylan in Minnesota, Paul Butterfield in Chicago, John Lennon and Mick Jagger in England—all were sorting through these artifacts of a nearly forgotten subculture to form a dominant new cultural expression of their own.

The music of bluesman Jimmy Reed, for example, offered an alternative to the daily experience of "growing up absurd" (as Paul Goodman phrased it). When adolescence was given the form of Delta blues to articulate its woes, the resulting expression ran deeper than predictable teenage complaints. "Radio is where people hang out," Dylan said of these years, and the new music being discovered gave his generation unique resources from which to fashion their imaginations. Although black music (and concomitant cultural values) had made some impression on the larger

American culture during the twenties (through jazz) and the thirties (such as by Fletcher Henderson's writing for the Benny Goodman Orchestra and the popularity of Duke Ellington), its style had been kept apart from the mainstream since the end of World War II (think of the more conservative music of Sauter/Finnegan, who had been Glenn Miller's white arrangers, plus the more technical academic jazz of Woody Herman and Stan Kenton).

The most probing question contemporary radio could ask in 1957 was "How much is that doggie in the window?" Within five years, those same stations would be playing songs which asked "How many times must the cannonballs fly / Before they're forever banned?" No commercial medium in America's history had entertained such worries before. Even on a more personal level, the musical culture Bob Dylan chose spoke a more serious version of life. At night Dylan would hear Jimmy Reed singing about the gut issues of life and love which tended to be trivialized by so many elements of the dominant culture, from Patti Page to high school English. As an alternative to the daytime culture, Dylan could spend his nights listening to Leadbelly sing goodnight to Irene and in the next verse sometimes take a great notion to go down to the river and drown (a startling sentiment Ken Kesey found appropriate for the title and epigraph of his second sixties novel). Dylan learned that the traditional twelve-bar blues structure was a perfect vehicle for irony and dark humor, two sentiments popular radio failed to offer, but which seemed appropriate to his own life. One of his earliest numbers was the traditional "Corrina, Corrina," a simple state-ment of sexual absence and longing, where an initial fact would be repeated, with different shadings of chord and tone, to form a bitter irony, leading to a third-line challenge of order, a statement of the blues:

```
C7
I got a bird that whistles, I got a bird that sings.
F7                        C7
I got a bird that whistles, I got a bird that sings.
G7             F7       C7
I ain't got Corrina, life don't mean a thing.
```

This was the style of Jimmy Reed. To his simple statements and plaintive cries Dylan added the rinky-tink rhythm of Fats Domino, whose tight lines of close, internal rhyme (think of "I'm Walkin' ") gave Dylan a form for his humorous, incremental, mile-a-minute indictments of life and times ("It's Alright, Ma, I'm Only Bleedin' "). The final ingredient, which Dylan waited until the mid-sixties to adopt, was the high-powered beat of James Brown, Chuck Berry, and especially Bobby Blue Bland, who were also in-fluencing the Rolling Stones and other popular groups. "Subterranean

Homesick Blues'' fuses all three elements: the refrain of a modified twelve-bar blues; the tightly packed, accusing lines; and the solid, steady, upbeat rhythm of Southern commercial blues (captured best in Charlie Watts' hi-hat–striking rhythm and Keith Richard's machine-gun guitar in the Stones' version of Bobby Womack's ''It's All Over Now,'' which preceded Dylan's recording by less than a year). This number led off Dylan's first musically radical album, *Bringing It All Back Home* (1965), which shocked the folk-attuned ears of his public, but which in fact brought his music home to the rock style it must have had with his band in high school, back in Hibbing.

Middle-class comforts made it uniquely possible for young people like Bob Dylan to focus on their more personal problems of growing up. What some might call a selfish and spoiled generation was actually an economic age-group whose blessings were not all salutary. Their leisure led to a deep self-consciousness, plus an awareness of what material plenty cost in personal terms. Life was something to be examined, in a way their Depression-bred parents never imagined. To be fourteen years old and newly rich, all at the same time, is not an easy load to bear.

Hence the spectacle of a well-educated son of an appliance store owner singing Mississippi blues in the Minnesota north country is not as ridiculous as it seems. His parents' culture gave Dylan no words to express his feelings. The spectral music from Little Rock and Nashville did, and because of this it was to become in the next decade the dominant cultural style. Nelson Riddle and his Orchestra gave way to a lone singer and one unamplified guitar. Hence the disturbing range of Dylan's voice: all those grunts and snarls, screams and groans, compensating for the loss of strings and trombones. The singer would now express it all himself. And his message was abruptly personal. The commercial formulas of Tin Pan Alley were discarded for issues the slick materialistic culture had tried to efface with full employment and faultless mental hygiene. The complaints were valid, and the issues of Bob Dylan's songs would soon be demonstrated in the streets.

His first album, *Bob Dylan,* was recorded in October 1961, and draws heavily on the blues tradition. ''In My Time of Dyin' '' and ''Fixin' to Die'' rely as much on vocal quality as words to convey their message, as does the mournful sound of ''House of the Rising Sun.'' These songs follow the natural range of Dylan's voice, and reflect a personality consistent in his best material through the 1970s (as opposed to the pseudofolk posing of ''Talking New York Blues,'' a virtual requirement of the then-popular hootenanny and coffeehouse circuit Dylan counted on for early exposure). His debut song is ''You're No Good'' by Jesse Lone Cat Fuller, a contemporary musician Ronald Sukenick celebrates in his novel set within sixties counterculture, *98.6* (1975). The qualities Sukenick appreciated in Lone Cat

Fuller's style were the ones Dylan adopted as his own: the ability to adapt a wide variety of influences into a mode of personal expression; to have one's experience expressed directly in one's music; and above all to create the kind of art which balances many different elements, some of them contradictory, in one improvisational whole. Sukenick's novel shows how just such qualities created the 1960s, and Dylan's music, drawing from a range as broad as two centuries of American popular culture, works the same way.

Dylan's music is above all a living art. Valid folk blues can be written in the present day, in "the green pastures of Harvard University," as Dylan himself describes a much-admired song by Ric Von Schmidt, "Baby, Let Me Follow You Down." Its rhythms and cadences come from the very style in which Dylan walks down the street—shoulders hunched, hands stuffed into pockets, and grinning face, the typical slouch of the late fifties teenager pictured on the cover of his second album, *Freewheelin'*. His own "Song for Woody Guthrie" sidesteps the dangers of hero worship and premature archaeology by shifting all the myths and history about the dying folksinger so that they are measured from Dylan's position in Hibbing, even though the rest of this first album pretends that the young man is firmly settled in New York. Positively Main Street.

The weakest elements in Dylan's early work are found in his attempts to exploit a patently contemporary, commercial idiom, that of highly intellectual folk music. His breakthrough to fame happened when his song "Blowin' in the Wind" was recorded by Peter, Paul & Mary. It was the first big-selling song of protest, but its politics are vague and indefinite; its lofty notions of peace and justice do little to challenge immediate cultural standards, as do Dylan's later works which benefitted from a rock beat and more sharply pointed lyrics. But his failure is instructive, for it tells us just what would be effective in forming a new culture, and what would not. Indefinite gestures of revolt such as "Blowin' in the Wind" can be easily turned into verbal *Muzak,* its highly literary message anthologized with other sentiments conveniently ignored by the operating culture. But rock and blues "are where people hang out," as Dylan said, and when his work takes their style, his protest is more effective—just as the style of James Kunen's *The Strawberry Statement* tells us more about the truth of the student revolution than a dozen issue-oriented books.

The poetic side of Bob Dylan is more effective in "A Hard Rain's A-Gonna Fall," which manages to talk about the 1962 Cuban missile crisis without ever bringing up the subject, simply because there's no time. "Every line in it," Dylan revealed on the album's liner notes, "is actually the start of a whole song. But when I wrote it, I thought I wouldn't have enough time alive to write all those songs so I put all I could into this one," with the same style of personal inclusiveness Ronald Sukenick admired in Lone Cat Fuller. There is no linear continuity in "Hard Rain"; the images are highly individual and complex, yet exist for the listener all at once, since there is no convenient scheme for sorting them out afterward (Vonnegut would use the same strategy in *Slaughterhouse-Five*). One album, *The Times They Are A-Changin'* (1964), was sufficient to work this literary impulse out of Dylan's system. Half a year later *Another Side of Bob Dylan* (1964) reestablished the elemental nature of his blues, from honky-tonk piano ("Black Crow Blues") to simple rock and roll ("Motorpsycho Nitemare"). His best writing was now in such works as "My Back Pages," which boasted a strong melody and let the writer's feelings take expression in the singer's voice rather than in words. "It Ain't Me Babe" finds a musical structure for personal statement. Stronger statements called for stronger music, not more heavy literary references.

Given Dylan's growth, the move to hard rock was inevitable—either that or begin writing novels, for what he had to say could no longer be carried by the simple strum of folk guitar. That strum lasts just one bar into *Bringing It All Back Home* (1965). Dylan's Fender Stratocaster screams in at the second measure, a logical complement to his plaintive voice of the folk period, now calling a paranoiac warning to the counterculture in "Subterranean Homesick Blues." Its Rolling Stones tempo, with a tambourine atop the drummer's hi-hat striking each second and fourth beat with the regularity of a chain-gang hammer, drives home a four-image-to-the-measure catalogue of current fears: orders from the DA, trench-coated men from the government, and so forth. "Look out kid, there's something you did" is specific enough. Everybody gets the message. You don't need a weatherman to know which way the wind blows.

"She Belongs To Me" shows the same style can be adapted to more gentle material. It is a tender but tough love song, unaffected plain statement, in a twelve-bar blues structure with added chordal subtlety in the last four measures to indicate the singer's satisfaction and approval, rather than regret. "Maggie's Farm" is protest phrased in highly personal, musically organic forms, and "Bob Dylan's 115th Dream" is similarly composed of verbal riffs, this time drawn from six hundred years of American history, hilariously mixed up and packed into a twelve-bar blues. The album's second side eases off on the hard rock, but still relies on an absolute identity of voice and music; Dylan's voice on "Mr. Tambourine Man" gives no quarter, coming across as relentless as a musical instrument. Words themselves are massed as convincingly as symphonic themes in "It's Alright, Ma." The power of Dylan's pure lyricism makes "It's All Over

Now, Baby Blue'' an important statement of cultural value, without having to make one specific reference to the times, changing or not.

Highway 61 Revisited (1965) is a virtual anthology of rock influences, Dylan's proof that he had mastered the full vocabulary of American popular music. "Tombstone Blues" could be mistaken for a cut by the Rolling Stones, whose own work had synthesized Dylan's same sources. "It Takes a Lot to Laugh, It Takes A Train to Cry" uses the best of Jimmy Reed, as "From a Buick 6" takes the characteristic bass line and guitar riff from the work of Carl Perkins. "Tombstone Blues" and the more thoughtful "Desolation Row" mark another development in Dylan's language, as he uses a conventional narrative framework to create stories out of madly disparate elements. As a result, the song's form questions itself and achieves a double effect, giving the listener the best of both worlds of representation and abstraction.

By 1966 Dylan could be counted on to express the new culture's self-image as adequately as any poet or novelist, and his "Rainy Day Women No. 12 & 35" (from *Blonde on Blonde*) is the first evidence that protest could be a matter of simple good-time fun. Its exuberance comes from the black humor view toward oppression and intimidation, much in the manner of Kurt Vonnegut's *Cat's Cradle,* which was widely circulated in paperback among the counterculture that year. Song triumphs over protest—Dylan's singsong voice and his rowdy accompaniment guarantee it, much as the form of Bokonon's Calypsoes keeps the novel's religion from taking itself too seriously (and losing sight of its real purpose). Other material from this album covered the range of solid-pop idioms (again with blues roots, as "Pledging My Time") to the mastery of ballad lyrics, notably in "Just Like a Woman," where multiple, internal rhymes strengthened the song's effect. More often now Dylan preferred the urban blues sound Paul Butterfield had discovered among older black musicians on Chicago's South Side, and for one session he used Butterfield's first guitarist, Mike Bloomfield (himself a student of black urban blues). Blues rock was for now Dylan's appropriate form, and from June through October of 1967 he took time off to see how far this style could be extended (the public excuse was recovery from a minor injury when his motorcycle slipped on the backyard grass). Eventually released in 1975 as *The Basement Tapes,* this music provided Dylan with the most sophisticated rock backup he would ever have: his tour group The Hawks on their way to rehearsing themselves into The Band. With them as his laboratory and living workshop, Dylan could try his hand at commercial rock writing, such as "Odds and Ends" and especially "Long Distance Operator," a funky floor-tom romp through rhythms and changes The Coasters had popularized in "Searchin' " and other tunes in the early sixties. The Band themselves were experimenting with even older styles of Churck Berry and Gene Vincent ("Don't Ya Tell Henry" and "Yazoo Street Scandal"). But for them a more subtle, original style emerged from these sessions. Best expressed in Dylan's originals "Tears of Rage" and "This Wheel's on Fire," The Band's unique instrumental and vocal timber combined to form a sound no other group could copy, the essence of definitive style. Not even Dylan attempted it outside of these experimental sessions.

There are many explanations for the turn to country rock in the later years of the sixties, a style which was shared by musicians as distinctive as Bob Dylan, the Byrds, and the Buffalo Springfield. Some say it was a mellow withdrawal from the more strident aspects of counterculture life, which by now included the more bloody and sometimes fatal elements of protest. Others said it was an ironic comment on the times, which occasionally did seem like childish scraps between make-believe cowboys and Indians. One advantage Dylan saw was the chance to move back into a folk idiom, now less cumbersome with the lighter line and chordal subtlety of *John Wesley Harding* (1968). Its theme was vaguely messianic, which also fit the period. But intimations of Hank Williams and Johnny Cash are present on this album ("I'll Be Your Baby Tonight"), while even the rock number ("Down Along the Cove") is more in the style of another Nashville artist, Jerry Lee Lewis. So unlike the music of *The Basement Tapes,* this album was in fact a transition to Dylan's pure-country album, *Nashville Skyline* (1969), a mastery of virtually all the musical styles to come out of that city during the 1960s. From them Dylan culled his own creation, "Lay Lady Lay," which assumed most of Nashville's distinctive studio elements to shape a new voice and new musical personality to go with it. Dylan's final contribution to the decade, the massive *Self Portrait* double album released in 1970, runs the pop gauntlet from Hank Williams to Gordon Lightfoot. Less important than Bob Dylan is the music he addresses; the simple fact that he performs it shows how its styles and sentiments are compatible with the sixties aesthetic Dylan helped form.

Dylan's lasting importance, from his first recorded efforts at the top of the decade to his *Self Portrait* which closed it, is that he used his own musical personality to legitimize previously neglected or underrated musical styles—and to find within them the terms he needed to articulate a sense of the new, changing times. His own inventions, such as "Hard Rain," "It's Alright, Ma," and "Lay Lady Lay," are always in the space between existing styles. At a time when the sharpest aestheticians were questioning the idea of progress in the arts, Dylan showed how fresh music could emerge from discarded work. That new formulations of value were emerging at the same time reinforced the meaning of his music, which in turn helped show the way toward a new cultural model.

Neil Young's career begins in the country rock music Bob Dylan found satisfactory to close the decade of the sixties. His first group, the Buffalo Springfield, helped introduce the style in 1966. When the creative forces behind this music worked to fragment the group after 1968, Young became one of several figures (also from the Springfield were Stephen Stills, Richie Furay, and Jim Messina, and from other groups came David Crosby and Graham Nash) who sought personal identity by extending one feature or another of the same basic music. Of all these artists, Young has been the most persistent and most prolific. The quality of the eighteen albums on which he takes a major part indicates that, after Bob Dylan, he perfected the most interesting vocal and compositional style of the times.

Country rock, Young discovered, was a quieter and less cluttered idiom which allowed the same expressions of voice Bob Dylan had found in folk music earlier in the decade. Young's self-proclaimed "high squeaky voice" was not successful in a hard-rock format, and had been nearly smothered by the hard-driving instrumental work in some of the cuts on his first album, *The Buffalo Springfield* (1966), most notably in a song he wrote himself, "Burned." The music had to be toned down, with voice becoming the principal instrument, a situation much like Bob Dylan enjoyed when singing country blues back in 1961. But several years of hard-rock tradition needed to be transcended.

Neil Young's strategy was to put the voice up front, so high-pitched and mellow that drums and guitars virtually had to disappear so that the words could be heard. Yet literal meaning was not the point, because Young saw to it that once heard, the lyrics would not make conventional sense. His verbal absurdity surpassed even Dylan's; only Burton Cummings of the Guess Who (like Young, an emigré from Canada) came close, and he too was realizing that for voice to become a musical instrument it would have to be emptied of conceptual content—emptied of anything, in fact, which might distract from the singer's pure sound. "Nowadays Clancy Can't Even Sing" and "Flying on the Ground Is Wrong" are still heavy on accompaniment, but their lack of verbal pertinence or even intelligence keeps the voice from losing out; the melodic line Neil Young sings is far more important than what he sings about. A song, like an Abstract Expressionist painting or a piece of innovative fiction, should not be "about" anything else but itself, the sixties aesthetic had confirmed. Young's voice was complemented by his lead guitar work, which he used to fill in behind and especially between the lyrics. He preferred single-note statements as opposed to chords, phrased in blues style with a slight country twang; its most characteristic presence may be found in his accompaniment on Steve Stills' number, "For What It's Worth."

"Out of My Mind," written and sung by Neil Young, is his best performance on this first album and the clearest indication of his talents. He places his very vulnerable self at the center of the song, both as its singer and its composer. The squeaky highness of his voice becomes a positive asset, for he sets it against a world of threats and pressures (suggested by the band and surrounding voices) made all the more convincing by his sound of helpless culpability. The personal terror of alienation is Young's special contribution to the times, complemented by Steve Stills' contextually abstract but emotionally concrete cry of paranoia in "For What It's Worth," which in its vague suspicion of men with guns and danger in the streets reflected the rising tides of violence and intimidation the whole counterculture was experiencing. Far into his career Young would continue this style of writing and singing, ranging from "Helpless" on the Crosby, Stills, Nash, and Young *Déjà Vu* album of 1970 through the exquisite "Round and Round" from *Everybody Knows This Is Nowhere* (1969) and virtually all of the songs on what is probably his best collection, *After the Gold Rush* (1970).

The Buffalo Springfield's second album, *Again* (1967), departed from the two-minute/radio-tune format of their first LP and allowed Young to write more complete compositions. "Mr. Soul" is finished much in the Dylan manner, with incremental lines and close, internal rhymes. In this case the song's density comes from the rather simple device of writing three distinct (but rhymed) statements for each phrase of the twelve-bar blues, rather than repeating the first two according to tradition. The effect is that a lot more seems to be said. Even more holistic and overwhelming was the fact that Young still avoided easily conceptualized messages. His imagery is quite abstract, yet yielding a strong personal presence underscored by the song's compulsive rhythm and relentless prodding between phrases by his own lead guitar.

His quiet composition on this album is the song "Expecting to Fly," which complements the solitary voicing of "Out of My Mind" with the eerie, haunting string and synthesizer arrangements of Jack Nitzsche (who would contribute important scoring to Young's later albums). But the most startling work is "Broken Arrow," a six-minute composition (long for pop music even as late as 1967), which is one of Young's most surreal performances. Its combination of forms is so various that the piece itself becomes practically amorphous. It begins with the closing measures of "Mr. Soul," this time sung by drummer Dewey Martin in a funkier rhythm and blues fashion. The tune fades into a dreamlike lyric in Young's most slender and delicate voice, which tells a disconnected narrative montaged together from elements of rock-star life and nineteenth century encounters with Plains Indians. Crowd noises blend into hoots and shrieks from a circus calliope; rock-guitar riffs weave their way into the improvisations of jazz clarinet and piano; military drums are muffled into a heartbeat, all of which restate the song's musical theme, which carries the enigmatic question, "Did you see them?" repeated in each different context. What results is not a representational image but rather a piece of music existing as itself, or more properly as the record of its creator's activity in making it. In more conventional pieces, such as "Expecting to Fly," Young relied on Jack Nitzsche's arrangement to express the same wanderings of his consciousness which are more boldly depicted in "Broken Arrow."

Last Time Around (1968) was the Springfield's final album, a graphic representation of the paranoiac tendencies within the group itself which made it impossible for the members to work with each other, and which continued to plague the attempted reunions of Young and Stills throughout the seventies. But Neil Young was still growing as an artist. His major contribution to this last album was the song "I Am A Child," which places his self-consciously vulnerable voice within the complex chordal shadings of a quieter band. This richer musical sense carries over into his first solo album, *Neil Young* (1969). Although the initial tapes had to be remixed several times to keep Young's voice from disappearing completely beneath the instrumentation, the final product showed him in complete control of all musical elements. Much of the richness comes from Jack Nitzsche, whose hand is evident in most of the numbers. But the album as a whole has a deep compositional sense, something never possible among highly individualistic talents of the Buffalo Springfield. Central to the album's design are the instrumentals which lead off sides one and two: Young's "The Emperor of Wyoming" and Nitzsche's "String Quartet from Whiskey Boot Hill." The first is a happy pastoral idyll of Western guitar and strings, while Nitzsche's quartet uses sharp atonality to cast a spell of nervous unease. Young's remaining compositions follow the route thus described, until the last number finds an abstract resolution.

"The Loner" is the most starkly frightening song Young or any member of the Springfield has yet written. Guitar and organ refrains are used in a compositional manner, underscoring the heavy threats of Young's lyrics, which here use what may best be called "biomorphic" images— abstract forms suggesting vaguely human shapes, the perfect sense of a dark presence in an alley which is all the more dangerous because it's alive and can think. Young's voice is pitted against the heavy instrumentation, but when it wins, Nitzsche's strings are there to extend the lyricism. Unifying the piece is Young's habit of writing in four-stanza structures, with a subtle development in the imagery: each time the threat is made more insinuating. "The Old Laughing Lady" uses this same organization, enhanced by strange choral shadings of violins and eerie, disembodied voices (an example of biomorphic imagery in Nitzsche's work again). The album's final cut, "Last Trip to Tulsa," pushes the biomorphic into complete abstraction; by no coincidence, this song is also Young's most personal statement in the collection, again combining elements of stardom and human ecology. Like "Don't Let It Get You Down" from the later *Gold Rush* album, it is convincing on a much deeper level than "representation" can imply.

What Neil Young could accomplish within the laboratory of a working band is demonstrated on *Everybody Knows This Is Nowhere* (1969). The band was Crazy Horse, and like Dylan's Band it drew harder rock from country elements, coming full circle to the style Young had left in 1966, but now of his own making. Rock and roll was here to stay. "Down by the River" shows his control; his band gives him the framework for both vocal lyricism and expressive solo guitar work. Young's guitar now can extend implications of his voice, and he plays the instrument with the full authority of Keith Richard, Eric Clapton, and even Jimi Hendrix, complete to the power-distortion, pedal attachments, and pulled strings these musicians have used to make the electric guitar "speak." But Jack Nitzsche is still an important help, and in softer numbers like "Running Dry" he adds a solo violin which allows Young's voice to emerge directly from the music, rather than singing around it. *After the Gold Rush* (1970) capitalizes on this effect. The music is elemental, stripped down at times to pure voice. "Tell Me Why" uses just acoustic guitar and voices, while "After the Gold Rush" states its theme solely with Young's naked voice supported by his own simple piano chording. "Only Love Can Break Your Heart" uses a richer vocal chorus, but rhythmically phrased within the song's loping movement, so that there is no intrusive intellectual sense at all. Also in this album Young does much like Dylan in *Self Portrait*. He takes a well-known song from the more general popular culture, Don Gibson's "Oh, Lonesome Me," and by performing it with the same style as the rest of this very personal album, implies that his own vision is shared by a larger portion of the culture. Country rock always had this ideal, and by 1970 Dylan and Young were offering persuasive arguments that it could, at times, be true.

With his occasional colleagues Steve Stills, David Crosby, and Graham Nash, Neil Young contributed to the *Déjà Vu* album in 1970. His chief composition was typically complex, a three-part piece with the titles "Whiskey Boot Hill," "Down Down Down," and "Country Girl." Each has the same melody, but the underlying sounds are radically different. The first is rendered in Young's typically searching, straining voice, while the second deepens the sense of loss through abstract imagery. The sense of resolution in part three, "Country Girl," comes from an interesting device Young no doubt learned from Jack Nitzsche, though it was also used by James Taylor about the same time on "Knockin' Round the Zoo" (from his first album, *James Taylor*). In both songs, the final chord of a melody is turned minor by adding different notes in augmentation, creating a sense of ir-resolution, instability, and even outright fear. But just when we expect the passage to end, more notes are added in more radical augmentation until an entirely new, major chord is created, which forms the basis of a fresh melody.

But such compositions were really Neil Young's style for the sixties. As the seventies dawned, he discarded this sense of complexity for simple, good-time playing, a musical posture which could only have been earned by paying dues with more problematic forms. The simple hoe-down music of "Cripple Creek Ferry" which closes the *Gold Rush* album is a style Young would pursue through *Harvest* (1972) and beyond, including a song he wrote for Crazy Horse ("Dance, Dance, Dance") and in the performance of a number written by his close friend Danny Whitten of that band, "Come On Baby Let's Go Down Town." Musical structures were no longer threatening, intimidating affairs; serenity had been won.

Neil Young and Bob Dylan, then, began the 1970s with quite similar styles. Dylan's *New Morning* (1970) was just what its title implied, a reawakening from the dark night of sixties turmoil and uncertainty to sing plain popular music, which seemed all the more legitimate because it had been tempered and tested in the more difficult times before. Although some listeners complained that there were no more innovations, the early seventies were actually a rich musical period, where the disparate and distinctive styles of the previous decade were able to coexist and cross-fertilize. An easy lyricism was possible for such artists as James Taylor and Carole King, while the tougher musicians of the earlier period—Neil Young and Bob Dylan, Crazy Horse and The Band among them—were able to produce quality material within the widely various modes they had established in the late sixties. A Dylan concert or a Neil Young tour became a cultural and historical event, and audiences sensed the presence of an established *oeuvre* defining a shared period of struggle, to which a thousand candles would be lit at each performance.

Sixties Aesthetic

Art movements in the 1960s are as helpful as popular music in tracking the aesthetics of an age, for they respond to the same self-conscious notions of history. The path from Abstract Expressionism to Hard Edge to Minimal to Pop, Op, and Conceptual Art is as self-apparently progressive as the development in musical styles from folk to rock and country. The major topic of art in this century, most critics agree, has been its own art history. And not for reasons of aesthetic self-absorption—it has been the problematic nature of the times which causes art to examine itself, and in aesthetic terms, the sixties were the most problematic decade of them all. Music, fiction, poetry, cinema, theater, dance, and even the popularly expressive forms of anthropology showed evidence of such fruitful self-attention, making the times an intellectually active period to match the social turmoil encountered nearly every day. It is axiomatic that art reflects not life, but the imaginative conditions of life. Therefore imaginative upheavals can be traced by the seismographic upheavals in art, which in Western culture can be traced with great accuracy from the Middle Ages, at least.

In aesthetic terms, the sixties are the climax of trends active since the beginning of the century, and by the dawn of the seventies problems which date back to Picasso were starting to be solved. Only a major readjustment of cultural values could do that, but the almost frantically productive efforts of artists during these years suggest that such a revolution was indeed taking place. In the first decade of this century Cubism had prompted the overturn of half a millennium's view of the world by replacing the visual with the conceptual. There is a more complete way of picturing reality, argued Picasso and his colleagues during Cubism's first stage, than recording what one sees. The mind knows a fuller truth, which the illusions of painted vision obscure. The logic of this position is that the imagination is closer to life than any documentation available from the senses, and while the Cubists restricted this belief to painting (even its sculpture was half-hearted in comparison), subsequent movements worked toward extending this vision into the actual experience of life, until by the 1960s it constituted a new social ethic. The artistic act, as established in late Cubism (approximately 1914–1920), took on independent status. No longer would a picture be a representation of reality, a peculiar view of an artist who was expected to look at a landscape and see spheres, cones, and cylinders, or from a model's face perceive an arrangement of planes. The finished canvas was now an addition to that reality. And since it sprang from the artist's idea and not necessarily from something out there in nature, it was fundamentally creative, not re-creative.

Pictorial vision cannot help but operate in a long tradition, which in Western art reaches back to the mid-fifteenth century adoption of perspective. Cubism broke with this tradition, beginning an age of great personal freedom. Vision could not hope to tell the whole truth about experience, since it was limited to one level of epistemology and was fettered with a long history as well. Now Cubism invited the use of the sum total of sensations, coupled with creative intellect (still the most important element), so that in the end the artist's work would go far beyond the aesthetics of representation and become an active presence, an equivalent to life itself. Surrealism, with its contrary emphasis of the verbal, would momentarily disrupt this twentieth-century progression. For a time one major group of artistic thinkers, led by André Breton, suggested that the creative impulse could be reduced to a literary expression—hence the "readable" quality of canvases by Salvador Dali and some of Max Ernst. But Surrealism never took firm hold in America, where its principal exponent, Joseph Cornell, remained too much a romantic to sacrifice all to literacy. With the triumph of American painting in Abstract Expressionism, the goal of inciting a real event became primary, anticipating sixties fiction, poetry, and music, and the course of sixties art movements as well.

Getting the action on the canvas was the first step. This way the imagination would become primary, for both artist and viewer, since subjects could be evoked without resorting to description. Piet Mondrian's patterns of curves and lines, eventually yielding to just the straight lines themselves, sought directly for structure as visual experience. Paul Klee rejected even the lines, preferring the compositional sense of interlocking rectangular planes, using space and light for his experience. Through the twenties and thirties he moved toward more complex effects, including back-and-forth color actions (which anticipate Hans Hofmann), snarls of lines making roadmaps for the eyes (as would result from Jackson Pollock's drip method a decade later), and of pictographic emblems (foreshadowing the biomorphic images of even earlier Abstract Expressionism).

Joseph Cornell's work was even more dramatic. By incorporating personal objects, ready-made from the quotidian world, into three-dimensional boxes, he was able to create strikingly present enactments of his imagination at work. The objects in his boxes associated like the disparate events in dreams. Cornell enacts the chance encounters and odd coincidences which evoke principles of order and conjunction based mysteriously in the human imagination, which defy any literal translation. Donald Barthelme uses the same technique in his fictions and collage-stories, most particularly in his verbal assemblage, "Cornell," written for the Joseph Cornell retrospective at the Leo Castelli Gallery in 1976. In his novel *Moving Parts* (New York: Fiction Collective, 1977), Steve Katz uses his games with the number "43" to describe the appeal of such pseudosystems which Barthelme and Cornell use:

> These systems are tools useful to help you yourself arrive at a description of reality [in the anthropological, not artistic sense], but as soon as you depend on the system itself for the answers, start looking *at* it rather than *through* it, there begins to form a cataract of dogma over your perception of things as they are. (*43*, p. 22)

As system, it is uniquely self-destructive when misused; there is no danger, as with realism, that an expressive mode might be mistaken for anything more substantial than the convention it is. As for the mysterious resonances and teasing suspicions which make these works so inviting, Katz has an explanation. "It does seem relaxing to find that one of these systems works for us, because suddenly certain of our responsibilities for ourselves are taken off our heads for the moment, and we can give up some anxieties and get high" (*43*, p. 23). We have momentary control without the delusion that it means anything beyond aesthetic pleasure. Cornell's boxes are aesthetic pleasure machines, unique inventions which allow such enjoyment free of the rational and utilitarian considerations which ultimately push their way into such undertakings. The open spaces Cornell leaves are invitations for escape into infinity.

This aesthetic, which reaches from the earliest theories of Cubism to its greatest exercise in Abstract Expressionism (which in turn becomes the primary reflection of the culture), reverses the direction of Western art. Instead of the artist reaching outward toward a depiction of the world, he or she now looks inward, touching something in one's self. But not in a conventionally romantic sense. The soul is not about to be dug out and publicized. Instead a new reality is created, the form of which gives concrete expression to the idea, not a transformation of sensation. Once action and gesture are freed from the depiction of reality, they become part of experience themselves, and are worthy to have their own record enshrined as the work of art itself. The movement of intuition has been captured, for the viewer to reenact personally in the process of viewing the painting. The ultimate reality, then, is in the act of creation—a notion which elevates the graphic arts to the level of theology. As Harold Rosenberg made clear in his pioneering essay on "The American Action Painters," the canvas has now become an arena in which to act, rather than a space on which to reproduce.

The implications for other forms of art are astounding, as they should be for any such act of cultural re-creation. The key aesthetic principle is finding an answer to the problems of artistic expression, which date from Pablo Picasso and Georges Braque, in the truth of the medium itself—whether painting or poetry, film or dance. Clement Greenberg has argued that in times of challenge and crisis, painting sustains and strengthens itself by questioning its very being—by examining just what constitutes its essence, and discarding all the rest. What photography was to painting, at the beginning of the century, became in the sixties what news and information were to fiction, what television was to cinema, what the documentary was to theater.

The challenge to painting, however, resulted in an aesthetic doctrine adaptable to all the arts. Responding to the truth of the medium put a new emphasis on the materials of art, in place of the illusion they were formerly meant to convey. The artistic act then became the principal event, for all that was left was an encounter with materials. In painting, the canvas provided a field or ground for the track of the artist's energy, and the marks of that presence—stroke, brushmark, and drip—became the defining characteristics of Abstract Expressionism. Three decades' legacy has proven that this style of art was more than a glorification of technique; Jackson Pollock, for example, expressed an entire life on canvas, and an epic life at that. Even in terms of technique alone, operating within the truth of the canvas enriched the art of painting. As Harold Rosenberg has pointed out in *The Anxious Object* (New York: Horizon, 1966), Hans Hofmann as a teacher emphasized the student "learning how to organize forms behind one another on the single plane of the picture surface rather than causing them to recede through the illusory devices of perspective" (p. 147). The same enrichment of painting, Rosenberg adds, is evident in the color-field rectangles of Barnett Newman. That they "are real and living shapes means that they cannot be produced by external calculation but that the artist must enter into them as spatial indeterminates which he brings to certain dimensions in the experience of painting them, as one holds or cuts short an interval of breath" (p. 173).

Hofmann kept his action beneath the single plane of canvas surface as a way of expressing the truth of that canvas, for the illusion of depth demanded the willing suspension of disbelief which artists in all forms were rejecting as a style of make-believe story. There was also a moralism to be found: "Are we children reading fairy tales," asks Ronald Sukenick, "or men trying to work out the essentials of our fate?" His novel *Up* (1968) asserts that fact that "It's all words and nothing but words," just as Hofmann's technique insists that it's all paint and nothing but paint—applied, of course, with gesture (coincidentally, novelists such as Sukenick often included themselves as self-consciously creative characters, so that readers could see the words being put on the page).

The second stage of Abstract Expressionism, known as Color Field painting, was another step toward what has since become the sixties aesthetic. The work of Mark Rothko and then of Helen Frankenthaler reduced painting beyond the "object quality" of gesture (soon Robert Rauschenberg was to paint a typical "action-painting" brushstroke in his comic-strip dot technique to remind viewers of this inevitability). As opposed to the tracks and gestures left on the canvas by Pollock, de Kooning, and Kline, Rothko simply let large patches of color float before the viewer's eyes; Frankenthaler went farther by actually staining her canvases with a sponge. A trend was evident, from Color Field to Minimal and finally Conceptual Art: a steady reduction of reference to object.

To avoid objective reference in one's painting, yet still move beyond the gestural techniques of the Abstract Expressionists, became the great challenge to art in the sixties. The "combines" of Robert Rauschenberg adapted Abstract Expressionist action to ready-made objects; because the parts kept their own identity as objects from the real world, there was no danger that they might become referential objects within Rauschenberg's assemblage. Because there was no illusion, objects retained their integrity, just as they did in Pop Art. In fact, suspension of disbelief would ruin the work's effect. In similar manner, the serial art of Sol LeWitt, Larry Poons, Jasper Johns, and others was self-contained and nonreferential. Moreover, the nature of serial art argued against that ultimate posture of all referential work: the masterpiece. Painterly action, these younger artists showed, was feasible in ways other than the brushstroke, drip, or swirl.

Sixties sculpture developed in the same direction. Most representative were Claes Oldenburg's "soft sculptures," which became flamboyantly response oriented. The more traditionally hard forms of Tony Smith, Ron Bladen, and Barnett Newman drew their meaning not only from themselves but from the space they aggressively filled. In all cases, the viewer's participation in the work was paramount. The key artistic technique was a style of kinesthesis, which demanded that the audience take part in the work's creation and presence. Museum-as-mausoleum was finished as a concept; instead, performance (by the creator and then by the viewer) was the hallmark of contemporary art.

Op Art was a momentary, technical attempt to incorporate the viewer's actual mechanics of seeing, and followed directly in the sixties trend. But the major movement, dominant in the decade's later years, was Conceptual Art. Here the effacement of object was complete. Art would no more be something to look at than fiction would be a story to be told. Instead, the focus was on the conceptual activity of making art itself, as opposed to the traditional object-centered business of making, seeing, and appreciating. Concept replaced anecdote and emotion, and art became no longer the classification of objects but rather a record of the intellectual acts of the artist. Evolving art history became pure process, for now art could influence other art in terms of pure definition; the artwork itself was considered residue. Like the Dadaists and Surrealists of the 1920s, sixties artists courted a style of violence to wipe the slate clean. But they also valued wit and humor for the same ends, and their resulting manifestos and polemics stand as constructive acts against Dada's nihilistic bent toward destruction. The same joy and even exuberance fills the Conceptual Art of the sixties which we find in the decade's fiction, poetry, and popular music.

The sixties aesthetic is the climax of a trend which has rearranged the roles of artwork and audience. The work itself is now conditioned by location, such as Bladen's or Smith's room-filling sculptures. In the case of Dan Flavin's light sculpture, location actually helps create the work. Place dictates form, says Carl Andre; Christo adds that the work must become part of the environment, just as the environment is part of the work. In terms of the artistic act itself, the sixties make a turnabout of the modernist dictum that only the general can reflect the universal. Now we see that only the most personally expressive work can hint at the universal. As far as the viewer, our era demands participation on all levels, most emphatically in the creation of the artwork itself; by the time the process is complete, all senses are engaged in the multiform reality which the contemporary artwork has become. There is no room for illusion. Experience is more valued than simulation, which is, after all, counterfeit experience. The massive scale of sculpture reaches out to its public, competing with sixties architecture and technology. The artwork is now uniquely animated, as by its presence (whether as a massive Bladen sculpture or an Andy Warhol soup can) it experiences itself. Even dance joins the movement; the works of Yvonne Ranier suggest that action—what one *does*—is more important than character, attitude, plot, or any of the Aristotelian conventions. Ultimately, Conceptual Art presents the whole idea, without confusion. Art speaks to us in the immediacy of its creation.

Such enrichment of technique was a product of art's reductive testing, but was not the end in itself. The true personal benefit was to let the artist live in his or her paintings—think of Jackson Pollock taking his canvas off the easel and tacking it to the floor so he could literally dance within it, and getting rid of his brush so that nothing stood between himself and the paint. The viewer, in turn, is asked to participate in the making of the art object, re-creating it as vision follows the tracks of composition. By the 1960s poets in similar manner found out what was unique to their work and used it for the expression of lives of poetry (consider Frank O'Hara's "The Day Lady Died" as discussed in Chapter Three), and the novel was rescued from premature death by letting the fictionist live within his own book. Ronald Sukenick writing *Up* is perfectly analogous to Jackson Pollock painting "Full Fathom Five" (1947), and the reading of *Up,* whose only story is that of its own composition, is similar to viewing Pollock's work. In theater, the Happening creates itself, with audience participation; indeed, the line between spectator and creator is effectively erased, where the materials of dramatic art become living bodies placed in a theater building and little more (an effective use of these materials for full drama is Peter Handke's *Offending the Audience* [1966], a work with countless American equivalents). Dance submits to its own reality, discarding the toe shoes which defied gravity in favor of the bare feet which accommodate it, and attention is given to relating the body-in-motion with its environment, a physical transcription of Jackson Pollock's dance with the canvas. The most abrupt change is in film. Norman Mailer creates *Maidstone* (1968-1971) by taking forty hours of film as the equivalents of words, with which he "writes a film" by cutting and editing until an abstract work, bearing little factual pertinence to the scenes originally photographed, is produced. The ultimate form is a strict definition of materials: film not as moving photographs projected on a screen, but rather as a stencil passing before a beam of light twenty-four times per second. The frame is film's unique element. Even the camera may be dispensed with.

Each form of art, then, becomes a radically full experience as a result of its respective aesthetic challenge. What first threatened to be a loss or even extinction, as some painters feared when confronted with the camera, became the way to great enrichment. Less is definitely more. Hofmann's push and pull created a deeper surface than four hundred years of depth perception had allowed, and Sukenick's refusal to tell stories wound up telling a greatest story of all. Imagination was given a new primacy, all the more legitimate because a death-defying purge of art had proven its own naked possibility.

The popularity during the sixties of Carlos Castaneda's *The Teachings of Don Juan/A Yaqui Way of Knowledge* (Berkeley: University of California Press, 1968) and his subsequent volumes reflect just how this aesthetic had permeated the larger culture. In an age of self-help books, Castaneda was showing a way toward the ultimate personal improvement: living one's life as a creative venture, as an act of imagination within the field of one's environment. Certain primitive people, Castaneda suggested, were in closer touch with the totality of their world because of their versatility of perception; no single way of looking at things could dominate. Anthropology itself was the closest discipline civilized man could find to this pluralistic perception, for by examining different descriptions of reality, the anthropologist could sense the multiform nature of existence and perhaps even trace his way to the deep structure of human reality, or so the hopes of Claude Lévi-Strauss and others suggest.

But Castaneda makes no gestures toward deep structures. He is more concerned with day-to-day living in the world. His sorcerer-teacher Don Juan is as wary of perceptual tradition as was Pablo Picasso, and many of the old man's lessons are reminders that what his student receives as the world is merely a description of it "that has been pounded into me from the moment I was born," much as the Renaissance painters conditioned subsequent artists to view their subjects. Also, the simple description of life must be discarded in favor of revealing the truth of experience—just the formula Ronald Sukenick provides for innovative fiction. Castaneda describes this act as "stopping the world," calling a halt to having one's provisional view of things pass as absolute. The joy of conventions, Kurt Vonnegut has argued, is that they may be changed so freely, as long as we remember that they are conventions; but once habit transforms them into rules, our freedom becomes slavery.

As a sorcerer, Don Juan performs the same act as Frank O'Hara the poet, Ronald Sukenick the novelist, or Robert Rauschenberg the artist: to disarrange our perceptions of the familiar, so that our inhibitions fall away and we can see things freshly. In the difference between how things seemed before and how they appear now, in that magical, undefined space, is an approximation of how things may actually be. As anthropologist Walter Goldschmidt wrote in his Foreword to the first Castaneda volume, "By experiencing other worlds . . . we see our own for what it is and are thereby enabled to see fleetingly what the real world, the one between our own cultural construct and those other worlds, must in fact be like." Art deconditions us, Sukenick adds, "so that we may respond more fully to experience." To be real, that response must be in the form of an artistic act, to literally create the world we live in. Anything else is beside the point.

Authenticity is the key word for aesthetics in the sixties, describing everything from Conceptual Art to hard-rock music. In the late fifties, younger painters came to distrust one element of Abstract Expressionism, that the personal gestures enshrined in canvases by Jackson Pollock, Franz Kline, Willem de Kooning and the other masters would themselves assume the presence of subject matter, the very thing art had to discard in order to exist. Hence the movement toward Minimal Art, which sought a unified perception of mass, weight, and structure in its art objects as a way of avoiding the painterly elements of the older school. Its products aspired toward the almost purely holistic, exploiting the style behind a Mark Rothko color-field painting rather than the action painting of Pollock or Kline. Pure presence, in and of itself, now replaced act. The striking objects of the Hard Edge painters—Kenneth Noland's chevrons, for example— dominated the canvas, and a bit later in the sixties Pop Art proved, with some flamboyance, that an ample supply of hard edges were available everywhere within the larger art of the media (in the process giving added thought to "man in his environment"). The more pre-formed the object the better, given the suspect nature of gesture once Abstract Expressionism entered the museums. The development of Conceptual Art tried to insure that nothing could be bought, sold, speculated on, or enshrined. As an extreme application of Abstract Expressionism's purest aesthetic, it respected only the creator's mental activity in coming to a work; the work itself was beside the point, a souvenir or historical curiosity. "Art 'lives' through influencing other art," claimed Joseph Kosuth, most radical of the Conceptualists, "not by existing as the physical residue of an artist's ideas." Art is not necessarily something to look at—the greatest possible rejection of Picasso's first nemesis. Nor is fiction something that must tell a story. And so on through all the arts.

The transposition from "sincerity" to "authenticity" which Morris Dickstein has described in *The Gates of Eden* (1977) characterizes the intellectual politics of the sixties and carries over into the popular arts as well. The motivation can be traced to a basis in threat, in the deepest intimidation: that the quality of life to which Americans were accustomed was no longer liveable. But such a threat had been central to the arts since the century's beginning, and answered to the same solution—of discarding extraneous elements not only so the self might be preserved, but so that its essentials might be found and used to better and richer effect. In the process, previously undiscovered elements of American culture were found to be central to the decade's imagination: black music, environmental values, and ultimately an entirely new notion of the self. What began as matters of social pressure and turmoil in every case resulted in a new aesthetic definition and a virtual artistic renaissance: from the essays of Malcolm X to the innovative fiction of Ishmael Reed, from the Vietnam war reports of David Halberstam to the imaginative reactions of Michael Herr, and from the critical state of the graphic arts to the riot of sensations in Robert Rauschen-berg.

Ultimate causes for these imaginative changes can only be matter for speculation, but there are some guesses which fit the observable pattern of artistic life in the sixties. For one, there was the loss of credibility in assumed descriptions of order, or even in the ability to describe at all. The entire twentieth century had experienced this loss in terms of scientific knowledge or religious belief, but in the sixties it became a popular American phenomenon bearing directly on daily life. Whether fueled by civil rights or student protest, age-old domestic notions of order were challenged, and the destruction of Kennedy, the fall of Johnson, and the deterioration of Nixon undermined a conditioned faith in national leadership as well. On a personal level, habits were reconditioned by new demands of personal freedom. And on all levels of life priorities were rearranged; if not within one's own life, then on the TV screen, in the neighborhood, and even at home—the period's most popular weekly series, *All in the Family,* capitalized on just such situations and precipitated them further. No wonder imaginative acts by our best artists reflected the need for change.

On a higher level, it became evident as the sixties closed that the "last frontier" was not outer space but rather the human mind. By analogy, there seemed less interest in subject matter, and more in expression; content would yield to the act of creation itself, for this was the clue to the human intelligence which suddenly interested us more than aerobatics on the moon. With so many physical changes impending, Americans came to better trust their imaginations. New circumstances demanded it, and by discarding so much, a new culture discovered how much more had always been theirs.

INDEX